KITCHEN LIBRARY
Appetizers

KITCHEN LIBRARY
Appetizers

JANE PRICE

FALL RIVER PRESS

contents

THE PERFECT STARTING POINT	7
SOUPS	8
SALADS AND VEGETABLES	64
SEAFOOD	116
MEAT AND POULTRY	170
PASTA, GNOCCHI AND RICE	208
PASTRY	256
INDEX	298

The Perfect Starting Point

If you are contemplating serving an appetizer, chances are you are planning a dinner or lunch party. Not many of us make more than one course for a regular family dinner although sometimes we might offer a simple salad or soup as a prelude to a weekday main course — and sometimes, when appetites are flagging, certain appetizer dishes make the perfect light meal.

With *Kitchen Library Appetizers* as your resource, you'll never be at a loss when planning a menu. From quiche to quail, tarts, timbales, tortellini, and terrines, the starter for every occasion is now conveniently at your fingertips. This collection makes the business of choosing a particular appetizer easy for the cook. If it's an elegant occasion you're hosting, look no further than the delicious seafood options, all perfect preludes to a red meat or poultry main course. In warmer weather, a slice of seafood terrine, a pretty stack of marinated seafood, or slices of homemade gravlax with mustard sauce will entice with their clean, cool flavors. Watercress and duck salad with lychees, or prosciutto, camembert and fig salad are equally excellent choices to serve before a seafood-based main dish, and their clever combinations of ingredients are worthy of any restaurant menu.

An appetizer sets the tone for everything that's to follow and its success will both raise expectations and awaken appetites. It needs to be satisfying, without being too filling, and its flavors should balance well with the rest of your menu. It should look attractive and appealing, be in tune with the season and, most importantly for the cook, it needs to easily co-ordinate with the preparation and serving of the main course. With so many things to consider, it's timely that *Kitchen Library Appetizers* brings together a fabulous assemblage of every first course recipe you could ever wish for or imagine.

soups

Red Gazpacho

🌺 PREPARATION TIME: 40 MINUTES

🌺 COOKING TIME: NIL

2 lb 4 oz vine-ripened tomatoes

2 slices day-old white Italian bread,
    crust removed, broken into pieces

1 medium red bell pepper, seeded,
    membrane removed and roughly
    chopped

2 medium garlic cloves, chopped

1 small green chili, chopped, optional

1 teaspoon sugar

2 tablespoons red wine vinegar

2 tablespoons extra virgin olive oil

8 ice cubes

GARNISH

1/2 small cucumber, seeded
    and finely diced

1/2 medium red bell pepper, seeded,
    membrane removed and finely diced

1/2 medium green pepper, seeded,
    membrane removed and finely diced

1/2 medium red onion, finely diced

1/2 medium ripe tomato, diced

Score a cross in the base of the tomatoes. Put in a heatproof bowl and cover with boiling water. Leave for 30 seconds, then transfer to cold water and peel the skin away from the cross. Cut the tomatoes in half, scoop out the seeds and roughly chop.

Soak the bread in cold water for 5 minutes, then squeeze out any excess liquid. Put the bread in a food processor with the tomato, pepper, garlic, chili, sugar, and vinegar, and process until combined and smooth.

With the motor running, add the oil to make a smooth creamy mixture. Season to taste. Refrigerate for at least 2 hours. Add a little extra vinegar, if desired.

To make the garnish, mix all the ingredients in a bowl. Put two ice cubes in each bowl of soup and serve the garnish in separate bowls.

Garlic, Pasta and Fish Soup

❧ SERVES 4–6
❧ PREPARATION TIME: 30 MINUTES
❧ COOKING TIME: 40 MINUTES

⅓ cup olive oil
1 leek, white part only, trimmed and sliced
20–30 garlic cloves, thinly sliced
2 potatoes, chopped
8 cups fish stock
½ cup small pasta shapes
10 pattypan squash, halved
2 zucchini, cut into thick slices
10½ oz firm white fish fillets, chopped
    into large pieces
1–2 tablespoons lemon juice
2 tablespoons shredded basil

Heat the oil in a large saucepan, add the leek, garlic, and potato, and cook over medium heat for 10 minutes. Add 2 cups of the stock and cook for 10 minutes. Allow to cool slightly before transferring to a food processor or blender and blending, in batches, until smooth.

Pour the remaining stock into the pan and bring to the boil. Add the pasta, squash, and zucchini. Add the purée, and simmer for 15 minutes. When the pasta is soft, add the fish pieces and cook for 5 minutes, or until tender. Add the lemon juice and basil, and season to taste.

French Onion Soup

❧ SERVES 4–6
❧ PREPARATION TIME: 20 MINUTES
❧ COOKING TIME: 1 HOUR 45 MINUTES

¼ cup butter
6 onions (about 2 lb 4 oz), sliced into rings
1 teaspoon sugar
3 tablespoons all-purpose flour
9 cups vegetable stock
1 baguette, cut into ½ inch slices
½ cup grated gruyère or cheddar cheese,
    plus extra, to serve

Melt the butter in a large saucepan. Add the onion and cook slowly over low heat for about 20 minutes, or until tender. Add the sugar and flour and cook, stirring, for 1–2 minutes until the mixture is just starting to turn golden. Add the stock and bring to a simmer. Cover, and continue to cook over low heat for 1 hour, stirring occasionally. Season to taste.

Preheat the oven to 350°F. Bake the baguette slices for 20 minutes, turning once, until dry and golden. Top each slice with some of the grated cheese and place under a hot broiler until the cheese is melted. Serve the soup topped with the toasted cheese croutons. Sprinkle with extra grated cheese.

Garlic, Pasta and Fish Soup

Spicy Chicken Broth with Cilantro Pasta

- SERVES 4
- PREPARATION TIME: 1 HOUR
- COOKING TIME: 50 MINUTES

12 oz chicken thighs or wings, skin removed
2 carrots, finely chopped
2 celery stalks, finely chopped
2 small leeks, white part only, finely chopped
3 egg whites
6 cups chicken stock
Tabasco sauce

CILANTRO PASTA
½ cup all-purpose flour
1 egg
½ teaspoon sesame oil
2 cups cilantro leaves

Put the chicken pieces, carrot, celery, and leek in a large heavy-based saucepan. Push the chicken to one side and add the egg whites to the vegetables. Using a wire whisk, beat for a minute or so, until frothy (take care not to use a pan that can be scratched by the whisk).

Warm the stock in a separate saucepan, then gradually add the stock to the first pan, whisking continuously to froth the egg whites. Continue whisking while slowly bringing to a boil. Make a hole in the froth on top with a spoon and leave to simmer for 30 minutes, without stirring.

Line a large strainer with a damp dish towel or double thickness of cheesecloth and strain the broth into a clean bowl (discard the chicken and vegetables). Season with salt, pepper, and Tabasco sauce to taste. Set aside until you are ready to serve.

To make the cilantro pasta, sift the flour into a bowl and make a well in the center. Whisk the egg and oil together and pour into the well. Mix together to make a soft pasta dough and knead on a lightly floured surface for 2 minutes, until smooth.

Divide the pasta dough into four even portions. Roll one portion out very thinly and cover with a layer of evenly spaced cilantro leaves. Roll out another portion of pasta and lay this on top of the leaves, then gently roll the layers together. Repeat with the remaining pasta and cilantro.

Cut out squares of pasta around the leaves. The pasta may then be left to sit and dry out if it is not needed immediately. When you are ready to serve, heat the chicken broth gently in a pan. As the broth simmers, add the pasta and cook for 1 minute. Serve immediately.

Carrot and Cilantro Soup

- SERVES 4
- PREPARATION TIME: 15 MINUTES
- COOKING TIME: 1 HOUR 10 MINUTES

2 tablespoons olive oil
1 onion, chopped
1 lb 12 oz carrots, roughly chopped
1 bay leaf
1 teaspoon ground cumin
1 teaspoon cayenne pepper
1 teaspoon ground coriander
2 teaspoons paprika
5 cups chicken or vegetable stock
1 cup Greek-style yogurt
2 tablespoons chopped cilantro leaves, plus extra leaves, to garnish

Heat the oil in a saucepan, add the onion and carrot, and cook over low heat for 30 minutes. Add the bay leaf and spices, and cook for a further 2 minutes. Add the stock, bring to a boil, then reduce the heat and simmer, uncovered, for 40 minutes, or until the carrot is tender. Allow to cool slightly, before transferring to a food processor and blending, in batches, until smooth. Return to a clean saucepan and gently reheat. Season to taste.

Combine the yogurt and chopped cilantro in a bowl. Pour the soup into bowls and serve with a dollop of the yogurt mixture. Garnish with cilantro leaves.

Cream of Oyster Soup

- SERVES 4
- PREPARATION TIME: 15 MINUTES
- COOKING TIME: 20 MINUTES

18 fresh oysters, on the half shell
1 tablespoon butter
1 small onion, finely chopped
1/2 cup white wine
1 1/2 cups fish stock
1 cup whipping cream
6 whole black peppercorns
6 basil leaves, torn, plus extra, to garnish
1 teaspoon lime juice
scallions, shredded, to garnish

Drain the oysters in a small strainer and reserve the juice and oysters separately. Roughly chop six of the oysters. Melt the butter in a small saucepan and add the onion. Cover and cook over low heat until soft but not brown, stirring occasionally. Add the wine and simmer for 5 minutes, or until reduced by half.

Add the stock to the pan, simmer for 2 minutes, then add the cream, peppercorns, basil, and chopped oysters and simmer for 5 minutes. Strain, then push the mixture against the sides of the strainer, to extract as much flavor as possible. Discard the solids in the strainer.

Return the liquid to the pan and bring to a boil. Add the lime juice and reserved oyster juice. Season to taste. Spoon into four small bowls and add three oysters to each. Top with cracked black pepper. Garnish with scallions and basil.

Carrot and Cilantro Soup

Spicy Tomato and Pea Soup

✿ SERVES 6
✿ PREPARATION TIME: 15 MINUTES
✿ COOKING TIME: 20–25 MINUTES

6 large very ripe tomatoes, chopped
2 tablespoons ghee or butter
1 large onion, thinly sliced
1 garlic clove, crushed
2 teaspoons ground coriander
2 teaspoons ground cumin
1/2 teaspoon fennel seeds
2 bay leaves
1 green chili, seeded and sliced
1 1/2 cups coconut cream
1 1/2 cups frozen peas
1 tablespoon sugar
1 tablespoon chopped mint

In a saucepan, simmer the tomato in about 2 cups water until very tender. Allow to cool slightly before transferring to a food processor and blending, in batches, until smooth.

Heat the ghee in a large saucepan, add the onion and garlic, and cook over medium heat until very soft. Add the coriander, cumin, fennel seeds, bay leaves, and chili, and cook, stirring, for 1 minute. Add the coconut cream and the puréed tomatoes, and bring to a boil. Reduce the heat, add the peas and cook until tender. Remove the bay leaves, add the sugar and mint, and season with freshly ground pepper to taste.

New England Clam Chowder

✹ SERVES 4
✹ PREPARATION TIME: 35 MINUTES
✹ COOKING TIME: 45 MINUTES

3 lb 5 oz clams or pipis, in shell
2 teaspoons oil
3 medium bacon slices, chopped
1 medium onion, chopped
1 medium garlic clove, crushed
4 1/2 cups diced potatoes
1 1/4 cups fish stock
2 cups whole milk
1/2 cup whipping cream
3 tablespoons chopped Italian parsley

Discard any clams that are broken, already open or do not close when tapped on the bench. If necessary, soak in cold water for 1–2 hours to remove any grit. Drain and put in a large heavy-based saucepan with 1 cup water. Cover and simmer over low heat for 5 minutes, or until open. Discard any clams that do not open. Strain and reserve the liquid. Remove the clam meat from the shells.

Heat the oil in a clean saucepan. Add the bacon, onion, and garlic and cook, stirring, over medium heat until the onion is soft and the bacon golden. Add the potato and stir well.

Measure the reserved clam liquid and add water to make 1 1/4 cups. Add to the pan with the stock and milk. Bring to a boil, reduce the heat, cover and simmer for 20 minutes, or until the potato is tender. Uncover and simmer for 10 minutes, or until slightly thickened. Add the cream, clam meat, and parsley and season to taste. Heat through gently before serving, but do not allow to boil or the liquid may curdle.

Tomato Bread Soup (Pappa al Pomodoro)

🌿 SERVES 4
🌿 PREPARATION TIME: 25 MINUTES
🌿 COOKING TIME: 25 MINUTES

1 lb 10 oz vine-ripened tomatoes
1 loaf (about 1 lb) day-old crusty
    Italian bread
1 tablespoon olive oil
3 medium garlic cloves, crushed
1 tablespoon concentrated tomato purée
5 cups hot vegetable stock or water
1 tablespoon torn basil leaves
2–3 tablespoons extra virgin olive oil,
    plus extra, to serve

Score a cross in the base of the tomatoes. Put in a heatproof bowl and cover with boiling water. Leave for 30 seconds, then transfer to cold water and peel the skin away from the cross. Cut the tomatoes in half, scoop out the seeds and chop the flesh.

Discard most of the crust from the bread and tear the bread into $1^{1}/_{4}$ inch pieces.

Heat the oil in a large saucepan. Add the garlic, tomato, and tomato purée, then reduce the heat and simmer, stirring occasionally, for 10–15 minutes, or until reduced. Add the stock and bring to a boil, stirring for about 3 minutes. Reduce the heat to medium, add the bread pieces and cook, stirring, for 5 minutes, or until the bread softens and absorbs most of the liquid. Add more stock or water if the soup is too thick. Remove from the heat. Stir in the basil leaves and olive oil, and leave for 5 minutes so the flavors have time to develop. Drizzle with a little olive oil before serving.

Pasta and Bean Soup

🌿 SERVES 4–6
🌿 PREPARATION TIME: 20 MINUTES
🌿 COOKING TIME: 1 HOUR 25 MINUTES

$1^{1}/_{4}$ cups cranberry beans,
    soaked in water overnight
1 ham hock
1 medium onion, chopped
pinch ground cinnamon
pinch cayenne pepper
2 teaspoons olive oil
2 cups chicken stock
$4^{1}/_{2}$ oz tagliatelle (plain or spinach),
    broken into short lengths

Drain and rinse the cranberry beans, cover with cold water in a saucepan and bring to a boil. Stir, lower the heat and simmer for 15 minutes.

Drain the beans and transfer to a large saucepan with a tight-fitting lid. Add the ham hock, onion, cinnamon, cayenne, olive oil and stock, and enough cold water to cover. Cover and simmer over low heat for 1 hour, or until the beans are cooked and have begun to thicken the stock. Remove the hock and cut off any meat. Chop the meat and return it to the pan, discarding the bone. Season to taste.

When ready to serve, bring the soup back to a boil, toss in the tagliatelle and cook until *al dente*. Remove the pan from the heat and set aside for 1–2 minutes before serving.

Tomato Bread Soup (Pappa al Pomodoro)

Risoni and Mushroom Broth

SERVES 4

PREPARATION TIME: 15 MINUTES

COOKING TIME: 20–25 MINUTES

1/3 cup butter

2 medium garlic cloves, sliced

2 large onions, sliced

4 cups thinly sliced mushrooms

5 cups chicken stock

2/3 cup risoni

1 1/4 cups whipping cream

Melt the butter in a large saucepan over low heat. Add the garlic and onion and cook for 1 minute. Add the sliced mushrooms and cook gently, without coloring, for 5 minutes. (Set aside a few mushroom slices to use as a garnish.) Add the chicken stock and cook for 10 minutes. Allow to cool slightly before transferring to a food processor and blending until smooth.

Meanwhile, add the risoni in a large saucepan of rapidly boiling salted water and cook until *al dente*. Drain and set aside.

Return the soup to a clean pan and stir in the risoni and cream. Heat through and season to taste. Garnish with the reserved mushrooms.

Shrimp and Basil Soup

SERVES 4

PREPARATION TIME: 45 MINUTES

COOKING TIME: 15–20 MINUTES

1 lb 2 oz raw shrimp

2 tablespoons olive oil

1 1/2 tablespoons butter

2 medium garlic cloves

1 small red onion, thinly sliced

2 medium celery stalks, cut into thin
   batons

3 small carrots, cut into thin batons

1 tablespoon finely chopped Italian parsley

1 1/2 tablespoons finely chopped basil

pinch cayenne pepper

1/2 cup dry sherry

4 cups chicken stock

1/2 cup shell pasta

1/4 cup whipping cream

Peel the shrimp and gently pull out the dark vein from the back of each shrimp, starting from the head end.

In a large saucepan, heat the oil and butter. Add the garlic cloves and the onion and cook over low heat for 2–3 minutes. Add the celery and carrot and fry until the vegetables are golden, but not brown. Add the parsley, basil and cayenne pepper. Stir briefly, add the shrimp and toss through. Remove the garlic cloves. Pour in the sherry, increase the heat and cook for 2–3 minutes. Add the chicken stock, bring back to a boil, reduce the heat and simmer for 5 minutes. Add the shell pasta and simmer until the pasta is *al dente*. Stir in the cream and season to taste.

Risoni and Mushroom Broth

Crab and Corn Eggflower Noodle Broth

❋ SERVES 4

❋ PREPARATION TIME: 15 MINUTES

❋ COOKING TIME: 15 MINUTES

2$^1/_2$ oz dried thin egg noodles
1 tablespoon peanut oil
1 teaspoon finely chopped fresh ginger
3 medium scallions, thinly sliced,
    white and green parts separated
6 cups chicken stock
$^1/_3$ cup mirin
1$^1/_3$ cups fresh baby corn, sliced on the
    diagonal into $^1/_2$ inch slices
1 cup fresh crabmeat
1 tablespoon cornstarch mixed
    with 1 tablespoon water
2 eggs, lightly beaten
2 teaspoons lime juice
1 tablespoon soy sauce
3 tablespoons torn cilantro leaves

Cook the noodles in a large saucepan of boiling salted water for 3 minutes, or until just tender. Drain, then rinse under cold water. Set aside.

Heat a non-stick wok over high heat, add the peanut oil and swirl to coat the side of the wok. Add the ginger and white part of the scallions and cook over medium heat for 1–2 minutes. Add the stock, mirin and corn and bring to a boil, then simmer for 3 minutes. Stir in the noodles, crabmeat and cornstarch mixture. Return to a simmer and stir constantly until it thickens. Reduce the heat and pour in the egg in a thin stream, stirring constantly — do not boil. Gently stir in the lime juice, soy sauce and half the cilantro.

Divide the noodles among four bowls and ladle on the soup. Top with the green scallions and remaining cilantro leaves.

White Gazpacho (Ajo Blanco)

❋ SERVES 4–6

❋ PREPARATION TIME: 20 MINUTES

❋ COOKING TIME: 3 MINUTES

1 loaf day-old white Italian bread
1 cup blanched almonds
3–4 medium garlic cloves, chopped
$^1/_2$ cup extra virgin olive oil
$^1/_3$ cup sherry or white
    wine vinegar
1$^1/_2$ cups vegetable stock
2 tablespoons olive oil, extra
3 cups cubed day-old white Italian bread,
    extra, with crust removed
1 cup small seedless green grapes

Remove the crusts from the loaf of bread. Soak the bread in cold water for 5 minutes, then squeeze out any excess liquid. Chop the almonds and garlic in a food processor until well ground. Add the bread and process until smooth.

With the motor running, add the oil in a slow steady stream until the mixture is the consistency of thick mayonnaise. Slowly add the sherry and 1$^1/_4$ cups of stock. Blend for 1 minute. Season with salt. Refrigerate for at least 2 hours. The soup thickens on refrigeration so you may need to add the remaining stock or water to thin it.

When ready to serve, heat the extra oil in a frying pan, add the bread cubes and toss over medium heat for 2–3 minutes, or until golden. Drain on paper towel. Serve the soup very cold. Garnish with bread cubes and grapes.

Crab and Corn Eggflower Noodle Broth

Lobster Bisque

❀ SERVES 4–6

❀ PREPARATION TIME: 20 MINUTES

❀ COOKING TIME: 1 HOUR

1 raw lobster tail (about 14 oz)
1/3 cup butter
1 large onion, chopped
1 large carrot, chopped
1 medium celery stalk, chopped
1/4 cup brandy
1 cup white wine
6 medium parsley sprigs
1 medium thyme sprig
2 medium bay leaves
1 tablespoon concentrated tomato purée
4 cups fish stock
2 medium tomatoes, chopped
2 tablespoons rice flour or cornstarch
1/2 cup whipping cream

Remove the meat from the lobster tail. Wash the shell and crush into large pieces with a mallet or rolling pin, then set aside. Chop the meat into small pieces, cover and chill.

Melt the butter in a large saucepan, add the onion, carrot and celery and cook over low heat for 20 minutes, stirring occasionally, until the vegetables are softened but not brown.

In a small saucepan, heat the brandy, set alight with a long match and carefully pour over the vegetables. Shake the pan until the flame dies down. Add the white wine and the lightly crushed lobster shell. Increase the heat and boil until the liquid is reduced by half. Add the parsley, thyme, bay leaves, concentrated tomato purée, fish stock and chopped tomato. Simmer, uncovered, for 25 minutes, stirring occasionally.

Strain the mixture through a fine sieve or dampened cheesecloth, pressing gently to extract all the liquid. Discard the vegetables and lobster shell. Return the liquid to a cleaned pan.

Blend the rice flour or cornstarch with the cream in a small bowl. Add to the liquid and stir over medium heat until the mixture boils and thickens. Add the lobster meat and season to taste. Cook, without boiling, for 10 minutes, or until the lobster is just cooked. Serve hot.

NOTE: If you don't dampen the cheesecloth when straining the mixture, it will soak up too much of the liquid.

Winter Sqaush Soup with Harissa

SERVES 6
PREPARATION TIME: 10–40 MINUTES
COOKING TIME: 25 MINUTES

5 lb 8 oz winter squash
3 cups vegetable stock
3 cups milk
sugar, to taste

HARISSA
9 oz fresh or dried red chilies
1 tablespoon caraway seeds
1 tablespoon coriander seeds
2 teaspoons cumin seeds
4–6 garlic cloves
1 tablespoon dried mint
1/2 cup extra virgin olive oil

Remove the skin, seeds and fibre from the winter squash and cut into pieces. Simmer, uncovered, in a large saucepan with the stock and milk for about 20 minutes, or until tender. Allow to cool slightly before transferring to a food processor, and blending, in batches, until smooth. Season with a little sugar and black pepper. Return to a clean saucepan and gently reheat until ready to serve.

To make the harissa, wearing rubber gloves, remove the stems of the chilies, split in half, remove the seeds and soften the flesh in hot water for 5 minutes (or 30 minutes if using dried). Drain and place in a food processor.

While the chilies are soaking, dry-fry the caraway, coriander, and cumin seeds in a frying pan for about 1–2 minutes, or until aromatic. Add the spices, garlic, mint, and 1 teaspoon salt to the food processor and, slowly adding the olive oil, process until a smooth, thick paste forms. Stir the harissa into bowls of soup.

Tom Kha Gai

🌸 SERVES 4
🌸 PREPARATION TIME: 20 MINUTES
🌸 COOKING TIME: 20 MINUTES

2 inch piece fresh galangal, thinly sliced
2 cups coconut milk
1 cup chicken stock
1 lb 5 oz boneless, skinless chicken breasts,
    cut into thin strips
1–2 teaspoons finely chopped red chili
2 tablespoons fish sauce
1 teaspoon unpacked brown sugar
1/4 cup cilantro leaves, plus extra,
    to garnish

Combine the galangal, coconut milk, and chicken stock in a saucepan. Bring to a boil, then reduce the heat and simmer over low heat for 10 minutes, stirring occasionally. Add the chicken and chili to the pan and simmer for 8 minutes. Add the fish sauce and sugar and stir to combine. Add the cilantro leaves and serve immediately, garnished with cilantro sprigs.

Yogurt Soup

🌸 SERVES 4–6
🌸 PREPARATION TIME: 15 MINUTES
🌸 COOKING TIME: 20 MINUTES

6 cups vegetable stock
1/3 cup short-grain white rice
1/3 cup butter
1/3 cup all-purpose flour
1 cup plain yogurt
1 egg yolk
1 tablespoon finely sliced mint leaves
1/4 teaspoon cayenne pepper

Put the stock and rice in a saucepan and bring to a boil over high heat. Reduce the heat to medium–low and simmer for 10 minutes, then remove from heat and set aside.

In another saucepan, melt 1/4 cup of the butter over low heat. Stir in the flour and cook for 2–3 minutes, or until pale and foaming. Gradually add the stock and rice mixture, stirring constantly, and cook over medium heat for 2 minutes, or until the mixture thickens. Reduce the heat to low.

In a small bowl, whisk together the yogurt and egg yolk, then gradually pour into the soup, stirring constantly. Remove from the heat and stir in the mint and 1/2 teaspoon salt.

Just before serving, melt the remaining butter in a small saucepan over medium heat. Add the cayenne pepper and cook until the mixture is lightly browned. Pour over the soup.

Tom Kha Gai

Garlic Fish Stew (Bourride)

🌸 SERVES 8

🌸 PREPARATION TIME: 25 MINUTES

🌸 COOKING TIME: 1 HOUR 10 MINUTES

CROUTONS

1 tablespoon butter

1 tablespoon olive oil

4 slices white bread, crusts removed and
    cut into ⅝ inch cubes

4 lb 8 oz assorted firm white fish
    fillets (such as bass, whiting and cod)

AÏOLI

5 egg yolks

4 medium garlic cloves, crushed

3–5 teaspoons lemon juice

1 cup olive oil

STOCK

⅓ cup olive oil

1 large onion, chopped

1 medium carrot, sliced

1 medium leek, white part only, chopped

1⅔ cups dry white wine

1 teaspoon dried fennel seeds

2 medium garlic cloves, bruised

2 bay leaves

1 large strip orange zest

2 medium thyme sprigs

To make the croutons, heat the butter and oil in a heavy-based frying pan. When the butter begins to foam, add the bread cubes and cook for 5 minutes, or until golden. Drain on crumpled paper towel. Set aside.

Fillet the fish (or ask your fishmonger to do it), reserving the heads and bones for the stock.

To make the aïoli, put 2 of the egg yolks, garlic and 3 teaspoons lemon juice in a food processor and blend until creamy. With the motor still running, slowly drizzle in the oil. Season and add the remaining lemon juice, to taste. Set aside until needed.

To make the stock, heat the olive oil in large saucepan or stockpot and add the onion, carrot and leek. Cook over low heat for 12–15 minutes, or until the vegetables are soft. Add the fish heads and bones, wine, fennel seed, garlic, bay leaves, orange zest, thyme, black pepper and ½ teaspoon salt. Cover with 8 cups water. Bring to a boil and skim off the froth. Reduce the heat and simmer for 30 minutes. Strain into a pot, crushing the bones well to release as much flavor as possible. Return to the heat.

Preheat the oven to 225°F. Cut the fish fillets into large pieces about 3½ inches long. Add to the stock and bring to a simmer, putting the heavier pieces in first and adding the more delicate pieces later. Poach for 6–8 minutes, until the flesh starts to become translucent and begins to flake easily. Transfer the fish pieces to a serving platter and moisten with a little stock. Cover with foil and keep warm in the oven.

Place 8 tablespoons of the aïoli in a large bowl and add the remaining 3 egg yolks, stirring constantly. Ladle a little stock into the aïoli mixture, blend well and return slowly to the rest of the stock. Stir continuously with a wooden spoon for 8–10 minutes over low heat, or until the soup has thickened and coats the back of a spoon. Do not boil or the mixture will curdle. To serve, scatter the croutons and fish pieces into individual bowls and ladle the stock over the top.

Pie~Crust Mushroom Soup

14 oz large mushrooms
1/4 cup butter
1 medium onion, finely chopped
1 medium garlic clove, crushed
1/4 cup all-purpose flour
3 cups chicken stock
2 tablespoons thyme leaves
2 tablespoons sherry
1 cup whipping cream
2 sheets frozen puff pastry, thawed
1 egg, lightly beaten

Preheat the oven to 400°F. Peel and roughly chop the mushrooms, including the stems.

Melt the butter in a large saucepan, add the onion and cook over medium heat for 3 minutes, or until soft. Add the garlic and cook for 1 minute. Add the mushrooms and cook until soft. Sprinkle with the flour and stir for 1 minute. Stir in the stock and thyme and bring to a boil. Reduce the heat and simmer, covered, for 10 minutes. Allow to cool slightly before transferring to a food processor and blending, in batches.

Return the soup to the pan, stir in the sherry and cream then pour into four ovenproof bowls (use small, deep bowls rather than wide shallow ones, or the pastry may sag into the soup).

Cut rounds of pastry slightly larger than the bowl tops and cover each bowl with pastry. Seal the pastry edges and brush lightly with the egg. Place the bowls on a baking sheet and bake for 15 minutes, or until golden and puffed.

Green Pea Soup

❀ SERVES 4–6
❀ PREPARATION TIME: 20 MINUTES
❀ COOKING TIME: 1 HOUR 40 MINUTES

1½ cups dried green split peas
2 tablespoons oil
1 medium onion, finely chopped
1 medium celery stalk, finely sliced
1 medium carrot, finely sliced
1 tablespoon ground cumin
1 tablespoon ground coriander
2 teaspoons grated fresh ginger
5 cups vegetable stock
2 cups frozen green peas
1 tablespoon chopped mint
yogurt or sour cream, to serve

Soak the split peas in cold water for 2 hours. Drain the peas well.

Heat the oil in a large heavy-based saucepan and add the onion, celery and carrot. Cook over medium heat for 3 minutes, stirring occasionally, until soft but not browned. Stir in the cumin, coriander and ginger, then cook for 1 minute. Add the split peas and stock to pan. Bring to a boil, then reduce the heat to low. Simmer, covered, for 1½ hours, stirring occasionally. Add the frozen peas to the pan and stir to combine.

Allow to cool slightly before transferring to a food processor and blending, in batches, until smooth. Return to a clean pan and gently reheat. Season to taste and then stir in the mint. Serve in bowls with a swirl of yogurt or sour cream.

Corn Chowder

❀ SERVES 8
❀ PREPARATION TIME: 15 MINUTES
❀ COOKING TIME: 30 MINUTES

⅓ cup butter
2 large onions, finely chopped
1 medium garlic clove, crushed
2 teaspoons cumin seeds
4 cups vegetable stock
2 medium potatoes, chopped
1 cup canned creamed corn
2 cups corn kernels
3 tablespoons chopped Italian parsley
1 cup grated cheddar cheese
2 tablespoons snipped chives, to garnish

Heat the butter in large heavy-based saucepan. Add the onion and cook over medium–high heat for 5 minutes, or until golden. Add the garlic and cumin seeds, cook for 1 minute, stirring constantly. Add the vegetable stock and bring to a boil. Add the potatoes and reduce the heat. Simmer, uncovered, for 10 minutes.

Add the creamed corn, corn kernels and parsley. Bring to a boil, then reduce the heat and simmer for 10 minutes. Stir through the cheese and season to taste. Heat gently until the cheese melts.

Serve immediately, sprinkled with the chives.

Green Pea Soup

Zuppa Di Cozze

SERVES 6

PREPARATION TIME: 25 MINUTES

COOKING TIME: 35 MINUTES

7 oz ripe tomatoes
2 lb 4 oz black mussels
2 tablespoons olive oil
2 tablespoons butter
1 leek, white part only, finely chopped
3 garlic cloves, crushed
pinch saffron threads
1 tablespoon finely chopped Italian parsley
1 small red chili, finely chopped
2/3 cup dry white wine

Score a cross in the base of each tomato. Place in a heatproof bowl and cover with boiling water. Leave for 30 seconds, transfer to cold water, drain and peel away the skin from the cross. Cut the tomatoes in half, scoop out the seeds and finely chop the flesh.

Scrub the mussels with a stiff brush and pull out the hairy beards. Discard any broken mussels, or open ones that don't close when tapped on the bench. Rinse well.

Heat the oil and butter in a large saucepan and cook the leek and garlic over low heat until the leek is soft but not brown. Add the saffron, parsley, and chili and cook, stirring, for 1–2 minutes. Increase the heat and add the wine. Bring to a boil and cook for about 1–2 minutes, then add the chopped tomato and 1 cup water. Cover and simmer for about 20 minutes.

Add the mussels to the pan and cook, covered, until they are opened. After 4–5 minutes, discard any unopened mussels. So the soup is not too crowded with shells, remove one third of the remaining mussels, remove the mussel meat and add to the soup. Discard the empty shells. Season to taste. Serve immediately with crusty bread.

Red Pepper Soup

🌸 SERVES 6

🌸 PREPARATION TIME: 20 MINUTES

🌸 COOKING TIME: 30 MINUTES

4 red peppers
4 tomatoes
¼ cup olive oil
½ teaspoon dried marjoram
½ teaspoon dried mixed herbs
2 garlic cloves, crushed
1 teaspoon mild curry paste
1 red onion, sliced
1 leek, white part only, sliced
9 oz green cabbage, chopped
1 teaspoon sweet chili sauce

Cut the peppers into quarters. Remove the seeds and membrane. Broil until the skin blackens and blisters. Place on a cutting board, cover with a dish towel and allow to cool before peeling and chopping.

Score a cross in the base of the tomatoes. Put in a heatproof bowl and cover with boiling water. Leave for 30 seconds, then transfer to cold water. Drain and peel the skin away from the cross. Cut the tomatoes in half, scoop out the seeds and chop the flesh.

Heat the oil in a large saucepan. Add the herbs, garlic, and curry paste. Stir over low heat for 1 minute, or until aromatic. Add the onion and leek and cook for 3 minutes, or until golden. Add the cabbage, capsicum, tomato, and 4 cups water. Bring to a boil, reduce heat, and simmer for 20 minutes. Remove from the heat.

Allow to cool slightly before transferring to a food processor and blending, in batches, for 30 seconds, or until smooth. Return the soup to a clean saucepan, stir through the chili sauce, and season to taste with salt and freshly ground black pepper. Reheat gently and serve hot.

Wild Rice Soup

❧ SERVES 6
❧ PREPARATION TIME: 15 MINUTES
❧ COOKING TIME: 1 HOUR

½ cup wild rice
1 tablespoon olive oil
1 onion, finely chopped
2 celery stalks, finely chopped
1 green pepper, seeded, membrane
    removed and finely chopped
4 bacon slices, finely chopped
4 large mushrooms, thinly sliced
4 cups chicken stock
½ cup whipping cream
1 tablespoon finely chopped Italian parsley

Put the wild rice in a saucepan with 2 cups water and bring to a boil. Cook for 40 minutes, or until the rice is tender. Drain and rinse well.

Heat the oil in a large saucepan and add the onion, celery, pepper and bacon. Fry for 8 minutes, or until the onion has softened and the bacon has browned. Add the mushrooms and cook for 1–2 minutes. Pour in the chicken stock and bring to a boil, then add the rice, stir, and cook the mixture for 2 minutes. Remove from the heat.

Stir in the cream and parsley, then reheat until the soup is almost boiling. Serve in deep bowls.

Watercress Soup

❧ SERVES 4–6
❧ PREPARATION TIME: 15 MINUTES
❧ COOKING TIME: 15–20 MINUTES

⅓ cup butter
1 onion, roughly chopped
4 scallions, roughly chopped
1 lb watercress, trimmed and roughly
    chopped
⅓ cup all-purpose flour
3 cups vegetable stock
sour cream or whipping cream, to serve

Melt the butter in a large saucepan and add the onion, scallion and watercress. Stir over low heat for 3 minutes, or until the vegetables have softened. Add the flour and stir until combined. Gradually add the stock and 1¼ cups water. Stir until smooth and the mixture boils and thickens. Simmer, covered, over low heat for 10 minutes, or until the watercress is tender.

Allow to cool slightly and transfer the mixture to a food processor and process, in batches, until smooth. Before serving, gently heat through and season to taste. Serve with a dollop of sour cream or cream.

Wild Rice Soup

Avgolemono Soup with Chicken

SERVES 4

PREPARATION TIME: 20 MINUTES

COOKING TIME: 30 MINUTES

1 onion, halved
2 whole cloves
1 carrot, cut into chunks
1 bay leaf
1 lb 2 oz boneless, skinless chicken breast
$\frac{1}{3}$ cup short-grain rice
3 eggs, separated
$\frac{1}{4}$ cup lemon juice
2 tablespoons chopped Italian parsley
4 thin lemon slices, to garnish

Stud the onion with the cloves and place in a large saucepan with 6 cups water. Add the carrot, bay leaf, and chicken, and season. Slowly bring to a boil, then reduce the heat and simmer for 10 minutes, or until the chicken is cooked.

Strain the stock into a clean saucepan, reserving the chicken and discarding the vegetables. Add the rice to the stock, bring to a boil, then reduce the heat and simmer for 15 minutes, or until the rice is tender. Meanwhile, tear the chicken into shreds.

Whisk the egg whites in a clean dry bowl until stiff peaks form, then beat in the yolks. Slowly beat in the lemon juice. Gently stir in about $\frac{2}{3}$ cup of the hot (not boiling) stock and beat thoroughly. Add the egg mixture to the stock and heat gently, but do not let it boil, otherwise the eggs may scramble. Add the chicken and season to taste.

Set aside for 2–3 minutes to allow the flavors to develop. To serve, spoon into bowls, sprinkle with parsley, and garnish with lemon slices.

Scallops with Buckwheat Noodles and Dashi Broth

❀ SERVES 4

❀ PREPARATION TIME: 10 MINUTES

❀ COOKING TIME: 15 MINUTES

9 oz dried buckwheat noodles
¼ cup mirin
¼ cup light soy sauce
2 teaspoons rice vinegar
1 teaspoon dashi granules
2 medium scallions, sliced
1 teaspoon finely chopped fresh ginger
24 large scallops (without roe)
5 fresh black fungus, chopped (see Note)
1 sheet nori, shredded

Add the noodles to a large saucepan of boiling water and stir to separate. Return to a boil, adding 1 cup cold water and repeat this step three times, as it comes to a boil. Drain and rinse under cold water.

Put the mirin, soy sauce, vinegar, dashi and 3½ cups water in a non-stick wok. Bring to a boil, then reduce the heat and simmer for 3–4 minutes. Add the scallions and ginger and keep at a gentle simmer.

Heat a chargrill pan or plate until very hot and sear the scallops in batches for 30 seconds each side. Remove from the pan. Divide the noodles and black fungus among four deep serving bowls. Pour ¾ cup of the broth into each bowl and top with six scallops each. Garnish with the shredded nori and serve immediately.

NOTE: If fresh black fungus is not available, use dried and soak it in warm water for 20 minutes.

Creamy Corn and Tomato Soup

🌺 SERVES 4–6
🌺 PREPARATION TIME: 20 MINUTES
🌺 COOKING TIME: 15 MINUTES

1 teaspoon olive oil
1 teaspoon bouillon powder
1 onion, finely chopped
3 tomatoes
15 oz concentrated tomato purée
11 oz canned creamed corn
4 1/2 oz canned corn kernels, drained
chili powder, to taste
sour cream and tortillas, to serve

Heat the oil in a large saucepan. Add the bouillon powder and onion and cook until the onion is soft.

Score a cross in the base of the tomatoes. Put in a heatproof bowl and cover with boiling water. Leave for 30 seconds, then transfer to cold water. Drain and peel the skin away from the cross. Cut each tomato in half, scoop out the seeds and chop the flesh.

Add the tomato to the pan with the tomato purée, creamed corn, and corn kernels. Season with chili. Stir until heated through. Serve with a dollop of sour cream and some warm tortillas.

Turkey and Corn Soup

🌺 SERVES 4
🌺 PREPARATION TIME: 10 MINUTES
🌺 COOKING TIME: 20 MINUTES

1 tablespoon butter
1 leek, white part only, thinly sliced
3 1/2 cups chicken stock
15 oz canned creamed corn
1 1/2 cups shredded cooked turkey

Melt the butter in a large saucepan, add the leek and stir over medium heat for 5 minutes, or until soft. Add the chicken stock and creamed corn and stir through. Season to taste. Bring to a boil, then reduce the heat and simmer, covered, for 5 minutes. Add the turkey to the pan and stir until heated through. Serve hot.

Creamy Corn And Tomato Soup

Lemon~Scented Broth with Tortellini

🌿 SERVES 4–6

🌿 PREPARATION TIME: 10 MINUTES

🌿 COOKING TIME: 20 MINUTES

1 lemon

1/2 cup white wine

15 1/2 oz canned chicken consommé

13 oz fresh or dried veal or chicken
    tortellini

4 tablespoons chopped Italian parsley

Using a vegetable peeler, peel wide strips from the lemon. Remove the white pith with a small sharp knife. Cut three of the wide pieces into fine strips and set aside for garnishing.

Combine the remaining wide lemon strips, white wine, consommé and 3 cups water in a large saucepan. Cook for 10 minutes over low heat. Remove the lemon zest from the pan and bring the mixture to a boil. Add the tortellini and parsley, and season with black pepper. Cook for 6–7 minutes, or until the pasta is *al dente*. Garnish with fine strips of lemon zest.

Garlic Soup

🌿 SERVES 4

🌿 PREPARATION TIME: 15 MINUTES

🌿 COOKING TIME: 45 MINUTES

1 garlic bulb

2 large thyme sprigs

4 cups chicken stock

1/3 cup whipping cream

4 thick slices white bread, crusts removed

thyme leaves, to garnish

Preheat the oven to 350°F. Crush the cloves (about 20) from the garlic bulb, using the side of a knife. Discard the skin and put the garlic in a large saucepan with the thyme sprigs, chicken stock, and 1 cup water. Bring to a boil, then reduce the heat and simmer, uncovered, for 20 minutes. Strain through a fine sieve into a clean saucepan. Add the cream and reheat gently without allowing to boil. Season to taste.

Meanwhile, cut the bread into bite-sized cubes. Spread on a baking sheet and bake for 5–10 minutes, or until lightly golden. Distribute among four soup bowls, then pour the soup over the bread. Garnish with thyme leaves and serve immediately.

Lemon-Scented Broth with Tortellini

Soup with Pesto (Soupe au Pistou)

❋ SERVES 8
❋ PREPARATION TIME: 45 MINUTES
❋ COOKING TIME: 35 MINUTES

2 medium ripe tomatoes
3 Italian parsley stalks
1 large rosemary sprig
1 large thyme sprig
1 large marjoram sprig
1/4 cup olive oil
2 medium onions, thinly sliced
1 medium leek, white part only, thinly sliced
1 medium bay leaf
2 1/2 cups winter squash, cut
    into small pieces
1 1/2 cups diced potato
1 medium carrot, halved lengthways and
    thinly sliced
8 cups vegetable stock or water
2/3 cup fresh or frozen fava beans
1/2 cup fresh or frozen peas
2 small zucchini, finely chopped
1/2 cup short macaroni or shell pasta

PESTO
3/4 cup basil leaves
2 large garlic cloves, crushed
1/3 cup olive oil
1/3 cup freshly grated parmesan cheese

Score a cross in the base of each tomato. Put in a heatproof bowl and cover with boiling water. Leave for 30 seconds then transfer to cold water, drain, peel away the skin from the cross and chop the flesh. Tie the parsley, rosemary, thyme and marjoram together with string.

Heat the oil in a heavy-based saucepan and add the onion and leek. Cook over low heat for 10 minutes, or until soft. Add the herb bunch, bay leaf, winter squash, potato, carrot, 1 teaspoon salt and the stock. Cover and simmer for 10 minutes, or until vegetables are almost tender.

Add the fava beans, peas, zucchini, tomatoes and pasta. Cover and cook for 15 minutes, or until the vegetables are very tender and the pasta is *al dente*. Add more water if necessary. Remove the herbs, including the bay leaf.

To make the pesto, finely chop the basil and garlic in a food processor. Pour in the oil gradually, processing until smooth. Stir in the parmesan and 1/2 teaspoon freshly ground black pepper and serve spooned over the soup.

NOTE: The flavor of this soup improves if refrigerated overnight then gently reheated.

Winter Squash, Shrimp and Coconut Soup

🌺 SERVES 4–6
🌺 PREPARATION TIME: 15 MINUTES
🌺 COOKING TIME: 20 MINUTES

1 lb 2 oz winter squash, diced
$1/3$ cup lime juice
2 lb 4 oz raw large shrimp
2 onions, chopped
1 small fresh red chili, finely chopped
1 lemon grass stem, white part only,
    chopped
1 teaspoon shrimp paste
1 teaspoon sugar
$1^1/2$ cups coconut milk
1 teaspoon tamarind purée
$1/2$ cup coconut cream
1 tablespoon fish sauce
2 tablespoons Thai basil leaves, plus extra,
    to serve

Combine the winter squash with half the lime juice in a bowl. Peel the shrimp and gently pull out the dark vein from each shrimp back, starting at the head end.

Process the onion, chili, lemon grass, shrimp paste, sugar, and $1/4$ cup coconut milk in a food processor until a paste forms.

Combine the paste with the remaining coconut milk, tamarind purée, and 1 cup water in a large saucepan and stir until smooth. Add the winter squash and lime juice to the pan and bring to a boil. Reduce the heat and simmer, covered, for 10 minutes, or until the squash is just tender.

Add the shrimp and coconut cream, then simmer for 3 minutes, or until the shrimp are just pink and cooked through. Stir in the fish sauce, the remaining lime juice, and the Thai basil leaves.

To serve, pour the soup into warmed bowls and garnish with basil leaves.

Tofu Miso Soup

⚘ SERVES 4

⚘ PREPARATION TIME: 10 MINUTES

⚘ COOKING TIME: 15 MINUTES

½ cup dashi granules

⅓ cup miso paste

1 tablespoon mirin

1⅓ cups cubed firm tofu

1 medium scallion, sliced, to serve

Using a wooden spoon, combine 4 cups water and the dashi granules in a small saucepan and bring to a boil.

Combine the miso paste and mirin in a small bowl, then add to the pan. Stir the miso over medium heat, taking care not to let the mixture boil once the miso has dissolved, or it will lose flavor. Add the tofu cubes to the hot stock and heat, without boiling, over medium heat for 5 minutes. Serve in individual bowls, garnished with the scallion.

Chinese Chicken and Corn Soup

⚘ SERVES 4

⚘ PREPARATION TIME: 10 MINUTES

⚘ COOKING TIME: 15 MINUTES

3 cups chicken stock

2 x 7 oz boneless, skinless chicken breasts

3–4 corn cobs

1 tablespoon vegetable oil

4 medium scallions, thinly sliced,
    white and green parts separated

1 medium garlic clove, crushed

2 teaspoons grated fresh ginger

1¼ cups canned creamed corn

2 tablespoons light soy sauce

1 tablespoon Chinese rice wine

1 tablespoon cornstarch

2 teaspoons sesame oil

Bring the stock to simmering point in a small saucepan. Add the chicken and remove the pan from the heat. Cover the pan and leave the chicken to cool in the liquid. Remove the chicken with a slotted spoon, then finely shred the meat using your fingers. Cut the corn kernels from the cobs — you should get about 2 cups of kernels.

Heat a wok over medium–high heat, add the oil and swirl to coat the side of the wok. Add the white part of the scallions, garlic and ginger and stir-fry for 30 seconds. Add the stock, corn kernels, creamed corn, soy sauce, rice wine and 1 cup water. Stir until the soup comes to a boil, then reduce the heat and simmer for 10 minutes. Add the chicken meat.

Meanwhile, stir the cornstarch, sesame oil and 1 tablespoon water together in a small bowl until smooth. Add a little of the hot stock, stir together, then pour this mixture into the soup. Bring to simmering point, stirring constantly for 3–4 minutes, or until slightly thickened. Season to taste. Garnish with the scallion greens.

Tofu Miso Soup

Creamy Red Lentil Soup

🌿 SERVES 6
🌿 PREPARATION TIME: 25 MINUTES
🌿 COOKING TIME: 1 HOUR

CROUTONS
4 thick bread slices, crusts removed
1/4 cup butter
1 tablespoon oil

1 1/2 teaspoons cumin seeds
1/3 cup butter
1 large brown onion, diced
3/4 cup red lentils, rinsed and drained
6 cups vegetable stock
2 tablespoons all-purpose flour
2 egg yolks
3/4 cup milk

To make the croutons, cut the bread into 1/2 inch cubes. Heat the butter and oil in a frying pan and when the butter foams, add the bread and cook over medium heat until golden and crisp. Drain on crumpled paper towel.

In a small frying pan, dry roast the cumin seeds until they start to pop and become aromatic. Leave to cool, then grind to a fine powder using a mortar and pestle.

Melt half the butter in a heavy-based saucepan and cook the onion over medium heat for 5–6 minutes, until softened. Add the lentils, ground cumin, and stock, and bring to a boil. Cover and simmer for 30–35 minutes, or until the lentils are very soft. Allow to cool slightly before transferring to a food processor and blending, in batches, until smooth.

In a large heavy-based saucepan, melt the remaining butter over low heat. Stir in the flour and cook for 2–3 minutes, or until pale and foaming. Stirring constantly, add the lentil purée gradually, then simmer for 4–5 minutes.

In a small bowl, combine the egg yolks and milk. Whisk a small amount of the soup into the egg mixture and then return it all to the soup, stirring constantly. Be careful not to boil the soup or the egg will curdle. Season to taste. Heat the soup to just under boiling and serve with the croutons.

Spinach and Lentil Soup

🌿 SERVES 4–6
🌿 PREPARATION TIME: 10 MINUTES
🌿 COOKING TIME: 1 HOUR 25 MINUTES

2 cups brown lentils
2 teaspoons olive oil
1 onion, finely chopped
2 garlic cloves, crushed
20 spinach leaves, stalks removed, leaves
    finely shredded
1 teaspoon ground cumin
1 teaspoon finely grated lemon zest
2 cups vegetable stock
2 tablespoons finely chopped cilantro

Put the lentils in a large saucepan with 5 cups water. Bring to a boil and then simmer, uncovered, for 1 hour. Rinse and drain, then set aside.

In a separate saucepan heat the oil. Add the onion and garlic. Cook over medium heat until golden. Add the spinach and cook for a further 2 minutes.

Add the lentils, cumin, lemon zest, vegetable stock, and 2 cups water to the pan. Simmer, uncovered, for 15 minutes. Add the cilantro and stir through. Serve immediately.

Won Ton Soup

🌿 SERVES 4–6
🌿 PREPARATION TIME: 40 MINUTES
🌿 COOKING TIME: 5 MINUTES

4 dried Chinese mushrooms
9 oz raw shrimp
9 oz ground pork
1 tablespoon soy sauce
1 teaspoon sesame oil
2 scallions, finely chopped, plus extra,
    sliced, to garnish
1 teaspoon grated fresh ginger
2 tablespoons canned chopped water
    chestnuts
9 oz package won ton wrappers
cornstarch, to dust
6 cups chicken or beef stock

Soak the mushrooms in a bowl of hot water for 30 minutes. Drain, then squeeze to remove any excess liquid. Discard the stems and chop the caps finely. Peel the shrimp, gently pulling out their dark veins. Finely chop the shrimp meat and mix in a bowl with the mushrooms, pork, soy sauce, sesame oil, scallion, ginger, and water chestnuts.

Cover the won ton wrappers with a damp dish towel to prevent them drying out. Working with one wrapper at a time, place a heaped teaspoon of mixture in the center of each. Moisten the pastry edges with water, fold in half diagonally, and bring the two points together. Place on a sheet dusted with cornstarch until ready to cook.

Cook the won tons in a saucepan of rapidly boiling water for 4–5 minutes.

In a separate saucepan bring the stock to a boil. Remove the won tons with a slotted spoon and place in serving bowls. Scatter the extra scallion over the top. Ladle the stock over the won tons.

Spinach and Lentil Soup

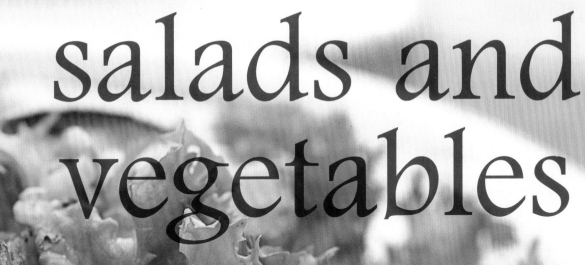

salads and vegetables

Tomato and Small Mozzarella Cheese Balls Salad

※ SERVES 4
※ PREPARATION TIME: 10 MINUTES
※ COOKING TIME: NIL

3 large vine-ripened tomatoes
1 2/3 cups fresh baby mozzarella cheese
   (bocconcini)
12 basil leaves
1/4 cup extra virgin olive oil

Slice the tomato into 12 1/2 inch slices. Slice the mozzarella cheese into 24 slices the same thickness as the tomato.

Arrange the tomato slices on a plate, alternating them with two slices of mozzarella cheese and placing a basil leaf between the cheese slices.

Drizzle with the olive oil and season well.

Shrimp and Cucumber Salad

※ SERVES 4
※ PREPARATION TIME: 20 MINUTES
※ COOKING TIME: 5 MINUTES

1 small cucumber, peeled
13 oz raw shrimp
1/4 cup rice vinegar
1 tablespoon sugar
1 tablespoon Japanese soy sauce
1 teaspoon finely grated fresh ginger
1 tablespoon white sesame seeds, toasted

Halve the cucumber lengthways and remove the seeds. Cut into thin slices, sprinkle thoroughly with salt and set aside for 5 minutes. Rinse to remove the salt and pat dry with paper towels. Put the shrimp in a saucepan of lightly salted boiling water and simmer for 2 minutes, or until just cooked. Drain, then plunge them into cold water. When the shrimp are cool, peel them, leaving the tails intact. Gently pull out the dark vein from the back of each shrimp, starting at the head end.

Put the vinegar, sugar, soy sauce and ginger in a large bowl and stir until the sugar dissolves. Add the shrimp and cucumber, cover and marinate in the refrigerator for 1 hour.

Drain the shrimp and cucumber from the marinade. Arrange on serving plates, sprinkle with the sesame seeds and serve.

Tomato and Small Mozzarella Cheese Balls Salad

Stuffed Artichokes

🌿 PREPARATION TIME: 1 HOUR 30 MINUTES
🌿 COOKING TIME: 1 HOUR 25 MINUTES

½ cup lemon juice
12 medium globe artichokes
2 cups ground lamb
½ cup fresh breadcrumbs
1 egg, lightly beaten
1 tablespoon chopped thyme
olive oil, for deep-frying
½ cup extra virgin olive oil
½ teaspoon ground turmeric
1 medium bay leaf
1½ cups chicken stock
3 tablespoons butter
2 tablespoons all-purpose flour

Fill a large bowl with water and add ¼ cup of the lemon juice. Peel the outer leaves from the artichokes, trimming the bases and stems to reveal the bases. Cut the tops off to reveal the chokes and remove the chokes. Put the artichokes in the bowl of acidulated water.

Put the lamb, breadcrumbs, egg and thyme in a bowl, season and mix well. Pat the artichokes dry with paper towels and fill each with 2 tablespoons of the lamb mixture.

Fill a deep-fryer or large heavy-based saucepan one-third full of olive oil and heat to 350°F, or until a cube of bread dropped into the oil browns in 15 seconds. Cook the artichokes in batches for 5 minutes, or until golden brown. Drain well.

Put the extra virgin olive oil, turmeric, bay leaf, remaining lemon juice and 1 cup of the stock in a 5-cup flameproof casserole dish. Season, then bring to a boil. Add the artichokes, reduce the heat, cover and simmer for 1 hour, or until tender, adding more stock if necessary. Turn the artichokes twice during cooking. Remove the artichokes and keep them warm. Reserve the cooking liquid.

Melt the butter in a saucepan, add the flour and stir for 1 minute, or until pale and foamy. Remove from the heat and gradually stir in the reserved cooking liquid. Return to the heat and stir until the sauce boils and thickens, then reduce the heat and simmer for 2 minutes. Serve immediately with the artichokes.

Salad Niçoise

✾ SERVES 4
✾ PREPARATION TIME: 30 MINUTES
✾ COOKING TIME: 15 MINUTES

3 eggs
2 medium vine-ripened tomatoes
1½ cups trimmed baby green beans
½ cup olive oil
2 tablespoons white wine vinegar
1 large garlic clove, halved
1½ oz iceberg lettuce heart
1 small red bell pepper
1 small cucumber
1 medium celery stalk
¼ large red onion, thinly sliced
1½ cups canned tuna, drained and broken
    into chunks
12 medium Kalamata olives
1½ oz canned anchovy fillets, drained
2 teaspoons baby capers, rinsed and
    squeezed dry
12 small basil leaves

Put the eggs in a saucepan of cold water. Bring to a boil, then reduce the heat and simmer for 10 minutes. Stir during the first few minutes to center the yolks. Cool under cold water, then peel and cut into quarters. Meanwhile, score a cross in the base of each tomato. Put in a heatproof bowl and cover with boiling water. Leave for 30 seconds, then transfer to cold water and peel the skin away from the cross. Cut each tomato into eight pieces.

Cook the beans in a saucepan of boiling water for 2 minutes, rinse under cold water, then drain.

Meanwhile, to make the dressing, whisk together the oil and vinegar.

Rub the garlic over the base and sides of a platter. Cut the lettuce into eight wedges and arrange over the base. Remove the seeds and membrane from the red pepper and thinly slice. Cut the cucumber and celery into thin 2 inch lengths. Layer the egg, tomato, beans, pepper, cucumber and celery over the lettuce. Scatter the onion and tuna over them, then the olives, anchovies, capers and basil. Drizzle with dressing and serve.

Fast Melon Salad

1 large honeydew melon

2 cups watercress sprigs, trimmed

2 avocados, sliced

1 large red pepper, thinly sliced

7¾ oz marinated feta cheese, crumbled
    into large chunks

½ cup marinated niçoise olives

DRESSING

¼ cup olive oil

2 tablespoons white wine vinegar

1 teaspoon dijon mustard

Cut the honeydew melon into slices and arrange on a large platter. Scatter the watercress sprigs over the top. Arrange the avocado, pepper, feta cheese, and niçoise olives on top.

To make the dressing, put the oil, vinegar, and mustard in a screw-top jar and shake until well combined. Drizzle over the salad.

Chef's Salad

DRESSING

½ cup extra virgin olive oil

2 tablespoons white wine vinegar

1 teaspoon sugar

1 iceberg lettuce

2 tomatoes, cut into wedges

2 celery stalks, cut into thin batons

1 cooked boneless, skinless chicken breast,
    cut into thin strips

7 oz ham, cut into thin strips

2¼ oz Swiss cheese, cut into strips

3 hard-boiled eggs, cut into wedges

6 radishes, sliced

Whisk the dressing ingredients together in a bowl until well combined. Season to taste.

Roughly shred the lettuce leaves and divide among serving plates. Top with layers of the tomato, celery, chicken, ham, cheese, egg, and radish. Drizzle the dressing over the salad and serve immediately.

Fast Melon Salad

Salmon and Fennel Salad

🌺 SERVES 4
🌺 PREPARATION TIME: 15 MINUTES
🌺 COOKING TIME: NIL

2 medium fennel bulbs
2 teaspoons dijon mustard
1 teaspoon sugar
½ cup olive oil
2 tablespoons lemon juice
7 oz smoked salmon, cut into strips
2 tablespoons snipped chives
1 tablespoon chopped dill, optional
arugula, to serve

Trim the fronds from the fennel. Slice the fennel bulbs and chop the fronds.

To make the dressing, whisk together the mustard, sugar, olive oil and lemon juice in a large bowl.

Add the sliced fennel bulb, salmon, chives and 1 tablespoon fennel fronds or dill to the bowl. Season and toss gently. Serve with the arugula and maybe some toast.

Stuffed Mushrooms

🌺 SERVES 4
🌺 PREPARATION TIME: 10 MINUTES
🌺 COOKING TIME: 25 MINUTES

8 large mushrooms
⅓ cup olive oil
¼ cup finely chopped prosciutto
1 medium garlic clove, crushed
2 tablespoons soft fresh breadcrumbs
⅓ cup freshly grated parmesan cheese
2 tablespoons chopped Italian parsley

Preheat the oven to 375°F. Lightly grease an ovenproof dish. Remove the mushroom stalks and finely chop them.

Heat 1 tablespoon of the oil in a frying pan, add the prosciutto, garlic and mushroom stalks and cook for 5 minutes. Mix in a bowl with the breadcrumbs, parmesan and parsley.

Brush the mushroom caps with 1 tablespoon of the olive oil and place them, gill side up, on the ovenproof dish. Divide the stuffing among the caps and bake for 20 minutes. Drizzle with the remaining oil and serve hot or warm.

Salmon and Fennel Salad

Russian Salad

❋ SERVES 4–6
❋ PREPARATION TIME: 40 MINUTES
❋ COOKING TIME: 40 MINUTES

MAYONNAISE
2 egg yolks
1 teaspoon dijon mustard
$^1/_2$ cup extra virgin olive oil
2 tablespoons lemon juice
2 small garlic cloves, crushed

3 canned globe artichoke hearts
3 waxy potatoes, such as desiree, unpeeled
$3^1/_2$ oz baby green beans, trimmed and cut
    into $^1/_2$ inch lengths
1 large carrot, cut into $^1/_2$ inch cubes
$^3/_4$ cup fresh peas
1 oz cornichons, chopped
2 tablespoons baby capers, rinsed and
    drained
4 anchovy fillets, finely chopped
10 black olives, cut into 3 slices
black olives, to garnish

To make the mayonnaise, beat the egg yolks with the mustard and $^1/_4$ teaspoon salt using electric beaters until creamy. Gradually add the oil in a fine stream, beating constantly until all the oil has been added. Add the lemon juice, garlic, and 1 teaspoon boiling water, and beat for 1 minute until well combined. Season, to taste.

Cut each artichoke into quarters. Rinse the potatoes, cover with cold salted water and bring to a gentle simmer. Cook for 15–20 minutes, or until tender when pierced with a knife. Drain and allow to cool slightly. Peel and set aside. When the potatoes are completely cool, cut into $^1/_2$ inch cubes.

Blanch the beans in boiling salted water until tender but still firm to the bite. Refresh in cold water, then drain thoroughly. Repeat with the carrot and peas.

Set aside a small quantity of each vegetable, including the cornichons, for the garnish, and season to taste. Put the remainder in a bowl with the capers, anchovies, and sliced olives. Add the mayonnaise, toss to combine, and season to taste. Arrange on a serving dish and garnish with the reserved vegetables and the whole olives.

NOTE: This salad can be prepared up to 2 days in advance and stored in the refrigerator but should be served at room temperature.

Asparagus with Citrus Hollandaise

🔥 SERVES 4
🔥 PREPARATION TIME: 15 MINUTES
🔥 COOKING TIME: 8 MINUTES

24 asparagus spears, woody ends trimmed
¾ cup butter
4 egg yolks
1–2 tablespoons lemon, lime or
    orange juice
shavings of parmesan or pecorino
    cheese (optional)

Put the asparagus in a saucepan of boiling water. Simmer for 2–4 minutes, or until just tender. Drain well.

Melt the butter in a small saucepan. Skim any froth from the top and discard. Allow the butter to cool.

Combine the egg yolks and 2 tablespoons water in a small saucepan and whisk for 30 seconds, or until pale and creamy. Place the pan over very low heat and continue whisking for 3 minutes, or until the mixture thickens. Remove from the heat. Add the cooled butter gradually, whisking constantly (leave the whey in the bottom of the pan). Stir in the lemon, lime or orange juice and season to taste. Drizzle the sauce over the asparagus and garnish with cheese shavings (if desired).

Mixed Vegetable Salad

🔥 SERVES 4–6
🔥 PREPARATION TIME: 40 MINUTES
🔥 COOKING TIME: 5 MINUTES

2 cups chopped pineapple
1 long cucumber, chopped
1⅔ cups cherry tomatoes, halved
1 cup sliced green beans
1¾ cups bean sprouts, trimmed
⅓ cup rice vinegar
2 tablespoons lime juice
2 red chilies, seeded and very finely
    chopped
2 teaspoons sugar
1 oz dried shrimp, to garnish
small mint leaves, to garnish

Toss together the pineapple, cucumber, tomatoes, beans, and sprouts in a bowl. Cover and refrigerate until chilled. Combine the vinegar, lime juice, chili, and sugar in a small bowl and stir until the sugar dissolves.

Dry-fry the shrimp in a frying pan, shaking the pan constantly until the shrimp are light orange and fragrant. Process the shrimp in a food processor until finely chopped.

Arrange the chilled salad on a serving platter, drizzle the dressing over the top, and garnish with the chopped shrimp and mint leaves. Serve immediately.

Asparagus with Citrus Hollandaise

Fish and Herb Salad

1 lb 2 oz smoked cod

¼ cup lime juice

½ cup flaked coconut

1 cup jasmine rice, cooked and cooled

¾ cup Vietnamese mint, chopped

3 tablespoons chopped mint

½ cup chopped cilantro leaves

8 kaffir lime leaves, very finely shredded

DRESSING

1 tablespoon chopped cilantro stem

¾ inch piece fresh ginger, finely grated

1 red chili, finely chopped

1 tablespoon chopped lemon grass, white part only

3 tablespoons chopped Thai basil

1 avocado, chopped

⅓ cup lime juice

2 tablespoons fish sauce

1 teaspoon unpacked brown sugar

½ cup peanut oil

Preheat the oven to 300°F. Put the cod in a large frying pan and cover with water. Add the lime juice and simmer for 15 minutes, or until the fish flakes when tested with a fork. Drain and set aside to cool slightly, before breaking it into bite-sized pieces.

Meanwhile, spread the coconut onto a baking sheet and toast in the oven for 10 minutes, or until golden brown, shaking the sheet occasionally. Remove the coconut from the sheet to prevent it burning.

Put the fish, coconut, rice, Vietnamese mint, mint, cilantro, and kaffir lime leaves in a large bowl and mix to combine.

To make the dressing, put the cilantro stem, ginger, chili, lemon grass, and basil in a food processor and process until combined. Add the avocado, lime juice, fish sauce, sugar, and peanut oil and process until creamy. Pour the dressing over the salad and toss to coat the rice and fish. Serve immediately.

Haloumi with Salad and Garlic Bread

- SERVES 4
- PREPARATION TIME: 20 MINUTES
- COOKING TIME: 5 MINUTES

4 firm tomatoes
1 small cucumber
4 cups arugula
$^1/_2$ cup kalamata olives
1 loaf crusty unsliced white bread
$3^1/_2$ fl oz olive oil
1 large garlic clove, halved
14 oz haloumi cheese
1 tablespoon lemon juice
1 tablespoon chopped oregano

Preheat the oven to 350°F. Heat the broiler to high.

Cut the tomatoes and cucumber into bite-sized chunks and place in a serving dish with the rocket and olives. Mix well.

Slice the bread into eight $^5/_8$ inch slices, drizzle $1^1/_2$ tablespoons of the olive oil over the bread, and season. Broil until lightly golden, then rub each slice thoroughly with a cut side of the garlic. Wrap loosely in foil and keep warm in the oven.

Cut the haloumi into eight slices. Heat 2 teaspoons of the oil in a shallow frying pan and fry the haloumi slices for 1–2 minutes each side, or until crisp and golden brown.

Whisk together the lemon juice, oregano, and remaining olive oil to make a dressing. Season to taste. Pour half the dressing over the salad and toss well. Arrange the haloumi on top and drizzle with the remaining dressing. Serve immediately with the garlic bread.

Crab and Mango Salad

2 x 1½ inch squares fresh coconut
1 teaspoon olive oil
2 cups trimmed watercress
1 cup snow pea sprouts
1 cup small cooked shrimp
2⅓ cups cooked fresh or canned
    crabmeat, drained if canned
1 firm medium mango, cut into thin strips
cilantro leaves, to garnish
1 medium lime, cut into slices, to garnish

DRESSING
⅓ cup light olive oil
¼ cup lime juice
1 teaspoon fish sauce
½ small green chili, finely chopped
1 tablespoon finely chopped cilantro leaves
2 teaspoons grated fresh ginger

To make the dressing, combine all the ingredients and season. Set aside to allow the flavors to infuse.

Peel the coconut into wafer-thin slices with a vegetable peeler. Heat the olive oil in a frying pan and gently fry the coconut, stirring, until golden. Drain on crumpled paper towels.

Combine the watercress and snow pea sprouts and arrange on a platter.

Peel the shrimp, leaving the tails intact. Gently pull out the dark vein from the back of each shrimp, starting at the head end. Lightly toss the crabmeat, shrimp, mango and three-quarters of the toasted coconut and dressing together. Stack in the center of the watercress and snow pea sprout mixture, scatter the remaining coconut over the top and garnish with the cilantro leaves and lime slices.

NOTE: If you can't get fresh coconut, use ½ cup flaked coconut and toast it.

Gado Gado

6 new potatoes

2 carrots, cut into batons

9 oz yard-long beans, trimmed and cut
   into 4 inch lengths

2 tablespoons peanut oil

9 oz firm tofu, cubed

2 cups baby spinach leaves

2 small cucumbers, cut into thick strips

1 large red pepper, cut into thick strips

1 cup bean sprouts, trimmed

5 hard-boiled eggs, cut in half

PEANUT SAUCE

1 tablespoon peanut oil

1 onion, finely chopped

$2/3$ cup peanut butter

$1/4$ cup kecap manis

2 tablespoons ground coriander

2 teaspoons chili sauce

$3/4$ cup coconut cream

1 teaspoon grated jaggery or unpacked
   brown sugar

1 tablespoon lemon juice

Cook the potatoes in a saucepan of salted boiling water until tender. Drain, cool slightly, then cut into quarters.

Cook the carrots and beans separately until just tender. Drain, plunge into iced water, then drain thoroughly.

Heat the oil in a non-stick frying pan and cook the tofu all over in batches until crisp. Drain on crumpled paper towels.

To make the peanut sauce, heat the oil in a frying pan over low heat and cook the onion for 5 minutes, or until golden. Add the peanut butter, kecap manis, ground coriander, chili sauce, and coconut cream. Bring to a boil, reduce the heat, and simmer for 5 minutes. Stir in the sugar and lemon juice, stirring until dissolved.

Arrange all the vegetables, tofu, and eggs on a plate around the bowl of peanut sauce.

Caesar Salad

🌿 SERVES 6

🌿 PREPARATION TIME: 25 MINUTES

🌿 COOKING TIME: 20 MINUTES

1 small baguette
2 tablespoons olive oil
2 medium garlic cloves, halved
4 medium bacon slices, trimmed of fat
2 medium romaine lettuces
10 anchovy fillets, halved lengthways
1 cup shaved parmesan cheese
parmesan cheese shavings, extra,
     to serve

DRESSING
1 egg yolk
2 medium garlic cloves, crushed
2 teaspoons dijon mustard
2 anchovy fillets
2 tablespoons white wine vinegar
1 tablespoon worcestershire sauce
¾ cup olive oil

Preheat the oven to 350°F. To make the croutons, cut the baguette into 15 thin slices and brush both sides of each slice with oil. Spread them on a baking sheet and bake for 10–15 minutes, or until golden brown. Leave to cool slightly, then rub each side of each slice with the cut edge of a garlic clove. The baked bread can then be broken roughly into pieces or cut into small cubes.

Cook the bacon under a hot broiler until crisp. Drain on paper towels until cooled, then break into chunky pieces.

Tear the lettuce into pieces and put in a large serving bowl with the bacon, anchovies, croutons and parmesan.

To make the dressing, place the egg yolk, garlic, mustard, anchovies, vinegar and worcestershire sauce in a food processor or blender. Season and process for 20 seconds, or until smooth. With the motor running, add enough oil in a thin stream to make the dressing thick and creamy.

Drizzle the dressing over the salad and toss very gently until well distributed. Sprinkle the parmesan shavings over the top.

Nachos with Guacamole

🪷 SERVES 4
🪷 PREPARATION TIME: 20 MINUTES
🪷 COOKING TIME: 5 MINUTES

15½ oz canned red kidney beans, rinsed
    and drained
2 cups ready-made tomato salsa
9 oz corn chips
2 cups grated cheddar cheese
⅓ cup sour cream

GUACAMOLE
1 scallion
1 small tomato
1 large avocado
1 tablespoon lemon juice

Preheat the oven to 350°F. Combine the kidney beans and ⅔ cup salsa, then divide the mixture between four ovenproof serving plates. Cover with corn chips and grated cheese. Put in the oven for 3–5 minutes, or until the cheese has melted.

To assemble, spoon the remaining salsa onto the melted cheese, then top with guacamole and sour cream.

To make the guacamole, finely chop the scallion and tomato. Cut the avocado in half, discard the skin, and stone. Mash the flesh lightly with a fork and combine with the scallion, tomato, lemon juice, and some freshly ground pepper.

Watercress and Duck Salad with Lychees

🌿 SERVES 4
🌿 PREPARATION TIME: 25 MINUTES
🌿 COOKING TIME: 30 MINUTES

2 large duck breasts, skin on
1 tablespoon soy sauce
1/2 each red, green and yellow pepper
8 cups watercress
12 fresh or canned lychees
2 tablespoons pickled shredded ginger
1–2 tablespoons green peppercorns
   (optional)
1 tablespoon white wine vinegar
2 teaspoons unpacked brown sugar
1–2 teaspoons chopped red chili
1 large handful cilantro leaves

Preheat the oven to 425°F. Brush the duck breasts with the soy sauce and put on a rack in a baking pan. Bake for 30 minutes. Remove from the oven and allow to cool.

Slice the peppers into thin strips. Discard any tough woody stems from the watercress. Peel the fresh lychees and remove the seeds. If you are using canned lychees, drain them thoroughly.

Arrange the pepper strips, watercress, lychees, and ginger on a large serving platter. Slice the duck into thin pieces and toss gently through the salad.

In a small bowl, combine the peppercorns, if using, vinegar, sugar, chili, and cilantro. Serve this on the side for spooning over the salad.

Prosciutto, Camembert and Fig Salad

🌿 SERVES 4
🌿 PREPARATION TIME: 10 MINUTES
🌿 COOKING TIME: 5 MINUTES

1/3 cup thinly sliced prosciutto
1 medium curly oak leaf lettuce
4 medium fresh figs, quartered
1/3 cup thinly sliced camembert cheese
1 medium garlic clove, crushed
1 tablespoon mustard
2 tablespoons white wine vinegar
1/3 cup olive oil

Cook the prosciutto under a hot broiler until crisp.

Arrange the lettuce leaves on a large plate and top with the figs, camembert and prosciutto.

Whisk together the garlic, mustard, vinegar and olive oil and drizzle over the salad.

Watercress and Duck Salad with Lychees

Green Papaya Salad

13 oz green papaya, peeled and seeded
3¼ oz yard-long beans, trimmed and cut
    into ¾ inch lengths
2 garlic cloves
2 small red chilies, chopped
5 teaspoons dried shrimp
8 cherry tomatoes, halved
1 cup cilantro sprigs
¼ cup chopped roasted peanuts
1 small red chili, sliced (optional)

DRESSING
¼ cup fish sauce
2 tablespoons tamarind purée
1 tablespoon lime juice
3 tablespoons grated jaggery or soft
    brown sugar

Grate the papaya, sprinkle with salt, and leave for 30 minutes. Rinse well.

Cook the beans in a saucepan of boiling water for 3 minutes, or until tender. Drain, plunge into cold water, then drain again.

To make the dressing, combine all ingredients in a small bowl. Set aside.

Pound the garlic and chili using a large mortar and pestle until crushed. Add the dried shrimp and pound until puréed. Add the papaya and snake beans and lightly pound for 1 minute. Add the tomato and pound briefly to bruise.

Combine the cilantro with the papaya mixture and spoon onto serving plates. Pour the dressing over the top. Sprinkle with the peanuts and, if desired, sliced red chili.

Cold Vegetable Salad with Spice Dressing

🌸 SERVES 4

🌸 PREPARATION TIME: 15 MINUTES

🌸 COOKING TIME: 5 MINUTES

10½ oz green or yard-long beans
10 spinach leaves
1 cup snow pea sprouts
1 red pepper
1 red onion
1 cup bean sprouts, trimmed

SPICE DRESSING
2 tablespoons peanut oil
1 garlic clove, crushed
1 teaspoon grated fresh ginger
1 small red chili, chopped
2 tablespoons dried coconut
1 tablespoon brown vinegar

Top and tail the beans and cut them into 4 inch lengths. Remove the stems from the spinach leaves and slice the leaves thinly. Remove about ½ inch of the long stems from the snow pea sprouts. Cut the pepper into thin strips. Thinly slice the onion.

Put the beans in a large saucepan of boiling water and cook for 1 minute to blanch, then drain. Combine the beans, spinach, snow pea sprouts, bean sprouts, pepper, and onion in a bowl.

To make the spice dressing, heat the oil in a small frying pan. Add the garlic, ginger, chili and coconut, and stir-fry over medium heat for 1 minute. Add the vinegar and ⅓ cup water, and simmer for 1 minute. Allow to cool.

To serve, add the dressing to the vegetables, and toss until combined.

NOTES: Snow pea sprouts are the growing tips and tendrils from the snow pea plant.
   Any blanched vegetables can be used in this salad. Try to use a variety of vegetables which result in a colorful appearance.
   The spice dressing can be added up to 30 minutes before serving.

Pork Noodle Salad

※ SERVES 4–6
※ PREPARATION TIME: 20 MINUTES
※ COOKING TIME: 35 MINUTES

BROTH
1 cup chicken stock
3 cilantro stems
2 kaffir lime leaves
1 1/4 inch piece fresh ginger, sliced

3 1/2 oz dried rice vermicelli
1 oz wood ear fungus (see Note)
1 small red chili, seeded and thinly sliced
2 red Asian shallots, thinly sliced
2 scallions, thinly sliced
2 garlic cloves, crushed
9 oz ground pork
1/4 cup lime juice
1/4 cup fish sauce
1 1/2 tablespoons grated jaggery or
   unpacked brown sugar
1/4 teaspoon ground white pepper
1 large handful cilantro leaves, chopped,
   plus extra, to serve
oakleaf or coral lettuce, to serve
lime wedges, to garnish
chili strips, to garnish

To make the broth, combine the stock, cilantro stems, kaffir lime leaves, ginger, and 1 cup water in a saucepan. Simmer for 25 minutes, or until the liquid has reduced to 3/4 cup. Strain and return to the pan.

Soak the vermicelli in a saucepan of boiling water for 6–7 minutes. Drain, then cut into 1 1/4 inch lengths. Discard the woody stems from the wood ear, then thinly slice. Combine the vermicelli, wood ear, chili, shallot, scallion, and garlic.

Return the broth to the heat and bring to a boil. Add the pork and stir, breaking up any lumps, for 1–2 minutes, or until the pork changes color and is cooked. Drain, then add to the vermicelli mixture.

In a separate bowl, combine the lime juice, fish sauce, jaggery, and white pepper, stirring until the sugar has dissolved. Add to the pork mixture along with the cilantro and mix well. Season with salt.

To assemble, tear or shred the lettuce, then arrange on a serving dish. Spoon the pork and noodle mixture on the lettuce and garnish with the lime wedges, chili and extra cilantro.

NOTE: Wood ear (also called black fungus) is a cultivated wood fungus. It is mainly available dried; and needs to be reconstituted in boiling water for a few minutes until it expands to five times its dried size, before cooking.

Panzanella

🔱 SERVES 6–8

🔱 PREPARATION TIME: 30 MINUTES

🔱 COOKING TIME: 5 MINUTES

1 small red onion, thinly sliced

9 oz stale bread such as ciabatta, crusts
    removed

4 ripe tomatoes

6 anchovy fillets, finely chopped

1 small garlic clove, crushed

1 tablespoon baby capers, rinsed, squeezed
    dry and chopped

2 tablespoons red wine vinegar

$1/2$ cup extra virgin olive oil

2 small cucumbers, peeled and sliced

$1/2$ cup basil leaves, torn

In a small bowl, cover the onion with cold water and leave for 5 minutes. Squeeze the rings in your hand, closing tightly and letting go, and repeating that process about five times. This removes the acid from the onion. Repeat the whole process twice more, using fresh water each time.

Tear the bread into rough $1\,1/4$ inch squares and toast lightly under a broiler for 4 minutes, or until bread is crisp but not browned. Allow to cool. Set aside.

Score a cross in the base of each tomato. Put in a heatproof bowl and cover with boiling water. Leave for 30 seconds, then transfer to cold water, drain and peel away the skin from the cross. Cut each tomato in half and scoop out the seeds. Roughly chop two of the tomatoes and purée the other two.

Combine the anchovies, garlic, and capers in a bowl. Add the vinegar and olive oil and whisk to combine. Season, then transfer to a large bowl and add the bread, onion, puréed and chopped tomato, cucumber, and basil. Toss well and season, to taste. Leave to stand for at least 15 minutes to allow the flavors to develop. Serve at room temperature.

Frisée and Garlic Crouton Salad

🌿 SERVES 4–6
🌿 PREPARATION TIME: 20 MINUTES
🌿 COOKING TIME: 10 MINUTES

1 tablespoon olive oil
1²/₃ cup speck, rind removed, cut into
    ¼ x ³/₄ inch pieces
½ baguette, sliced
4 medium garlic cloves
1 baby curly frisée
1 cup walnuts, toasted

VINAIGRETTE
1 medium French shallot, finely chopped
1 tablespoon dijon mustard
¼ cup tarragon vinegar
²/₃ cup extra virgin olive oil

To make the vinaigrette, whisk together the shallot, mustard and vinegar in a small bowl. Slowly add the oil, whisking constantly until thickened. Set aside.

Heat the oil in a large frying pan. Add the speck, bread and garlic and cook over medium–high heat for 5–8 minutes, or until the bread and speck are both crisp. Remove the garlic from the pan.

Put the frisée, baguette, speck, walnuts and vinaigrette in a large bowl. Toss together well and serve.

Tuna, Green Bean and Onion Salad

❀ SERVES 4
❀ PREPARATION TIME: 20 MINUTES
❀ COOKING TIME: 15 MINUTES

1²⁄₃ cups trimmed and sliced green beans
10½ oz penne rigate
½ cup olive oil
9 oz tuna steak, cut into thick slices
1 red onion, thinly sliced
1 tablespoon balsamic vinegar

In a large saucepan of boiling water, cook the beans for 1–2 minutes, or until tender but still crisp. Remove with a slotted spoon and rinse under cold water. Drain and transfer to a serving bowl.

Cook the pasta in a saucepan of boiling salted water until *al dente*. Drain, rinse under cold water, and drain again before adding to the beans.

Heat half the oil in a frying pan. Add the tuna and onion and gently sauté until the tuna is just cooked through. Stir the tuna carefully to prevent it from breaking up. Add the vinegar, increase the heat to high, and briefly cook until the dressing has reduced and lightly coats the tuna. Transfer the tuna and onion to a bowl.

Toss the beans, pasta, tuna, and onion together and mix with the remaining oil, and season to taste. Allow to cool before serving.

Shrimp and Papaya Salad with Lime Dressing

❀ SERVES 4

❀ PREPARATION TIME: 25 MINUTES

❀ COOKING TIME: NIL

1 lb 10 oz cooked shrimp
1 large papaya, chopped
1 small red onion, thinly sliced
2 celery stalks, thinly sliced
2 tablespoons shredded mint

LIME DRESSING
½ cup vegetable oil
¼ cup lime juice
2 teaspoons finely grated fresh ginger
1 teaspoon superfine sugar

Peel the shrimp, leaving the tails intact. Gently pull out the dark vein from each shrimp back, starting from the head end. Put the shrimp in a bowl.

To make the lime dressing, put the oil, lime juice, ginger, and sugar in a small bowl and whisk to combine. Season well.

Add the lime dressing to the shrimp and gently toss to coat the shrimp. Add the papaya, onion, celery, and mint and gently toss to combine. Serve the salad at room temperature, or cover and refrigerate for up to 3 hours before serving.

Fresh Beet and Goat's Cheese Salad

❀ SERVES 4

❀ PREPARATION TIME: 20 MINUTES

❀ COOKING TIME: 30 MINUTES

4 medium fresh beets, with leaves
1⅔ cup trimmed green beans
1 tablespoon red wine vinegar
2 tablespoons extra virgin olive oil
1 medium garlic clove, crushed
1 tablespoon capers, rinsed and squeezed
   dry, roughly chopped
¾ cup goat's cheese

Trim the leaves from the beets, scrub the bulbs and rinse. Put in a large saucepan of salted water, bring to a boil, reduce the heat, cover and simmer for 30 minutes.

Meanwhile, bring a saucepan of water to a boil, add the beans and cook for 3 minutes. Remove, plunge into cold water, and drain well. Add the beet leaves to the boiling water and cook for 3–5 minutes. Drain, plunge into a bowl of cold water, then drain well. Drain and cool the beets, peel the skins off and cut into thin wedges.

To make the dressing, mix the vinegar, oil, garlic, capers and ½ teaspoon each of salt and pepper. Divide the beans, beet leaves and bulbs among four serving plates. Crumble the goat's cheese over the top of each and drizzle with dressing. Delicious served with fresh crusty bread.

Shrimp and Papaya Salad with Lime Dressing

Chilled Buckwheat Noodles

SERVES 4

PREPARATION TIME: 25 MINUTES

COOKING TIME: 15 MINUTES

9 oz dried buckwheat noodles
$1\frac{1}{2}$ inch piece ginger
1 medium carrot
4 medium scallions, outside layer
   removed
1 sheet nori, to garnish
pickled ginger, to garnish
thinly sliced pickled daikon, to garnish

DIPPING SAUCE
3 tablespoons dashi granules
$\frac{1}{2}$ cup Japanese soy sauce
$\frac{1}{3}$ cup mirin

Put the noodles in a large saucepan of boiling water. When the water returns to a boil, pour in 1 cup cold water. Bring the water back to a boil and cook the noodles for 2–3 minutes, or until just tender — take care not to overcook them. Drain the noodles in a colander and then cool under cold running water. Drain thoroughly and set aside.

Cut the ginger and carrot into fine matchsticks about $1\frac{1}{2}$ inches long. Slice the scallions very finely. Bring a small saucepan of water to a boil, add the ginger, carrot and scallions and blanch for about 30 seconds. Drain and place in a bowl of iced water to cool. Drain again when the vegetables are cool.

To make the dipping sauce, combine $1\frac{1}{2}$ cups water, the dashi granules, soy sauce, mirin and a good pinch each of salt and pepper in a small saucepan. Bring the sauce to a boil, then cool completely. When ready to serve, pour the sauce into four small dipping bowls.

Gently toss the cooled noodles and vegetables to combine. Arrange in four individual serving bowls.

Toast the nori by holding it with tongs over low heat and moving it back and forward for about 15 seconds. Cut it into thin strips with scissors, and scatter the strips over the noodles. Place a little pickled ginger and daikon on the side of each plate. Serve the noodles with the dipping sauce. The noodles should be dipped into the sauce before being eaten.

Tomato and Basil Croustades

🌿 SERVES 4

🌿 PREPARATION TIME: 30 MINUTES

🌿 COOKING TIME: 20 MINUTES

1 day-old white bread loaf

3 tablespoons olive oil

2 garlic cloves, crushed

3 tomatoes, diced

9 oz fresh baby mozzarella cheese
   (bocconcini), cut into small chunks

1 tablespoon tiny capers, rinsed and dried

1 tablespoon extra virgin olive oil

2 teaspoons balsamic vinegar

4 tablespoons shredded basil

Preheat the oven to 350°F. Remove the crusts from the bread and cut the loaf into four even pieces. Using a small serrated knife, cut a square from the center of each cube of bread, leaving a border of about ⅝ inch on each side. You should be left with four 'boxes'. Combine the olive oil and garlic and brush all over the croustades. Place them on a baking sheet and bake for about 20 minutes, or until golden and crisp. Check them occasionally to make sure they don't burn.

Meanwhile, combine the tomato and bocconcini with the tiny capers in a bowl.

In another bowl, stir together the extra virgin olive oil and balsamic vinegar, then gently toss with the tomato mixture. Season with salt and freshly ground black pepper, then stir in the basil. Spoon into the croustades, allowing any excess to tumble over the sides.

Thai Beef Salad

❧ SERVES 6

❧ PREPARATION TIME: 20 MINUTES

❧ COOKING TIME: 5 MINUTES

1 lb 2 oz lean beef fillet

2 tablespoons peanut oil

2 medium garlic cloves, crushed

1 tablespoon grated jaggery
   or unpacked brown sugar

3 tablespoons chopped cilantro stems

1/3 cup lime juice

2 tablespoons fish sauce

1/4 teaspoon ground white pepper

2 small red chilies, seeded and
   thinly sliced

2 medium red Asian shallots, thinly sliced

2 long cucumbers, sliced into
   thin ribbons

2 large handfuls mint

1 cup trimmed bean sprouts

1/4 cup chopped toasted peanuts

Thinly slice the beef across the grain. Heat a wok over high heat, then add 1 tablespoon of the oil and swirl to coat the side of the wok. Add half the beef and cook for 1–2 minutes, or until medium–rare. Remove from the wok and put on a plate. Repeat with the remaining oil and beef.

Put the garlic, jaggery, cilantro, lime juice, fish sauce, pepper and 1/4 teaspoon salt in a bowl, and stir until all the sugar has dissolved. Add the chili and shallots and mix well.

Pour the sauce over the hot beef, mix together well, then allow the beef to cool to room temperature.

In a separate bowl, toss together the cucumber and mint, and refrigerate until required.

Make a stack of the cucumber and mint on a serving platter, then top with the beef, bean sprouts and peanuts.

Vegetable Pakoras

🌿 SERVES 4
🌿 PREPARATION TIME: 30 MINUTES
🌿 COOKING TIME: 20 MINUTES

RAITA
2 small cucumbers, peeled, seeded and
　　finely chopped
1 cup plain yogurt
1 teaspoon ground cumin
1 teaspoon mustard seeds
$\frac{1}{2}$ teaspoon grated fresh ginger
paprika, to garnish

$\frac{1}{3}$ cup chickpea flour
$\frac{1}{3}$ cup self-raising flour
$\frac{1}{3}$ cup soy flour
$\frac{1}{2}$ teaspoon ground turmeric
1 teaspoon cayenne pepper
$\frac{1}{2}$ teaspoon ground coriander
1 small green chili, seeded and finely
　　chopped
7 oz cauliflower
5 oz sweet potato
$6\frac{1}{4}$ oz eggplant
$6\frac{1}{4}$ oz asparagus, woody ends trimmed
vegetable oil, for deep-frying

To make the raita, mix the cucumber and yogurt in a bowl. Dry-fry the cumin and mustard seeds in a small frying pan over medium heat for 1 minute, or until fragrant and lightly browned, then add to the yogurt mixture. Stir in the ginger, season to taste, and mix together well. Garnish with paprika. Refrigerate until ready to serve.

Sift the chickpea flour, self-raising flour and soy flour into a bowl, then add the turmeric, cayenne pepper, ground coriander, chili, and 1 teaspoon salt. Gradually whisk in 1 cup cold water until a batter forms. Set aside for 15 minutes. Preheat the oven to 50°F.

Meanwhile, cut the cauliflower into small florets. Cut the sweet potato and eggplant into $\frac{1}{4}$ inch slices, and cut the asparagus into $2\frac{1}{2}$ inch lengths.

Fill a wok one-third full with the oil and heat to 325°F, or until a cube of bread dropped in the oil browns in 20 seconds. Dip the vegetables in the batter, then deep-fry them in small batches, for 1–2 minutes, or until pale golden. Remove with a slotted spoon and drain on crumpled paper towels. Keep warm in the oven until all the vegetables are cooked. Serve with the raita.

seafood

Oysters with Bloody Mary Sauce

🌿 SERVES 6
🌿 PREPARATION TIME: 20 MINUTES
🌿 COOKING TIME: NIL

24 oysters
¼ cup tomato juice
2 teaspoons vodka
1 teaspoon lemon juice
½ teaspoon worcestershire sauce
1–2 drops Tabasco sauce
1 medium celery stalk
1–2 teaspoons snipped chives

Remove the oysters from their shells. Clean and dry the shells. Combine the tomato juice, vodka, lemon juice, worcestershire sauce and Tabasco sauce in a small bowl.

Cut the celery stalk into very thin batons and place in the bases of the oyster shells. Top with an oyster and drizzle with tomato mixture. Sprinkle with the snipped chives.

Gravlax with Mustard Sauce

🌿 SERVES 12
🌿 PREPARATION TIME: 10 MINUTES
🌿 COOKING TIME: NIL

¼ cup sugar
2 tablespoons sea salt
1 teaspoon crushed black peppercorns
5 lb 8 oz salmon, filleted, skin on
1 tablespoon vodka or brandy
4 tablespoons very finely chopped dill

MUSTARD SAUCE
1½ tablespoons cider vinegar
1 teaspoon sugar
½ cup olive oil
2 teaspoons chopped dill
2 tablespoons dijon mustard

Combine the sugar, salt and peppercorns in a small dish. Remove any bones from the salmon with tweezers. Pat dry with paper towels and lay a fillet, skin side down, in a shallow sheet or ovenproof dish. Sprinkle the fillet with half the vodka, rub half the sugar mixture into the flesh, then sprinkle with half the dill. Sprinkle the remaining vodka over the second salmon fillet and rub the remaining sugar mixture into the flesh. Lay it, flesh side down, on top of the other fillet. Cover with plastic wrap, place a heavy board on top and then weigh the board down with three heavy cans or a foil-covered brick. Refrigerate for 24 hours, turning it over after 12 hours.

To make the mustard sauce, whisk all the ingredients together, then cover until needed.

Uncover the salmon and lay the fillets on a wooden board. Brush off the dill and seasoning with a stiff pastry brush. Sprinkle with the remaining dill, pressing it onto the salmon flesh, shaking off any excess. Serve whole on the serving board, or thinly sliced on an angle towards the tail, with the sauce.

NOTE: Gravlax can be refrigerated, covered, for up to a week.

Oysters with Bloody Mary Sauce

Marinated Seafood

🔱 SERVES 8

🔱 PREPARATION TIME: 40 MINUTES

🔱 COOKING TIME: 10 MINUTES

1 lb 2 oz raw shrimp

1 lb 2 oz mussels, scrubbed, beards removed

1/2 cup white wine vinegar

3 bay leaves

1 lb 2 oz small squid tubes, sliced

1 lb 2 oz cleaned scallops (without roe)

DRESSING

2 garlic cloves, crushed

1/2 cup extra virgin olive oil

1/4 cup lemon juice

1 tablespoon white wine vinegar

1 teaspoon dijon mustard

1 tablespoon chopped Italian parsley

Peel the shrimp, leaving the tails intact. Gently pull out the dark vein from each shrimp back, starting from the head end.

Discard any mussels that are already open. Put the vinegar, bay leaves, 3 cups water, and 1/2 teaspoon salt in a large saucepan and bring to a boil. Add the squid and scallops, then reduce the heat to low and simmer for 2–3 minutes, or until the seafood has turned white. Remove the squid and scallops with a slotted spoon and put in a bowl.

Repeat the process with the shrimp, cooking until just pink, then removing with a slotted spoon. Return the liquid to a boil and add the mussels. Cover, reduce the heat and simmer for 3 minutes, or until all the shells are open. Stir occasionally and discard any unopened mussels. Cool, remove the meat, and add to the bowl.

To make the dressing, whisk the garlic and oil together with the lemon juice, vinegar, mustard, and parsley. Pour over the seafood and toss well. Refrigerate for 1–2 hours before serving.

NOTE: Seafood should never be overcooked or it will become tough.

Crab Cakes with Avocado Salsa

2 eggs, lightly beaten
2 cups canned crabmeat, drained
1 medium scallion, finely chopped
1 tablespoon mayonnaise
2 teaspoons sweet chili sauce
1¼ cups fresh white breadcrumbs
oil, for pan-frying
lime wedges, to serve
cilantro leaves, to garnish

AVOCADO SALSA
2 medium plum tomatoes, chopped
1 small red onion, finely chopped
1 large avocado, diced
¼ cup lime juice
2 tablespoons chervil
1 teaspoon sugar

Combine the eggs, crabmeat, scallion, mayonnaise, sweet chili sauce and breadcrumbs in a bowl. Stir well and season. Using wet hands, form the crab mixture into eight small flat patties. Cover and refrigerate for 30 minutes.

To make the avocado salsa, put the tomato, onion, avocado, lime juice, chervil and sugar in a bowl. Season and toss gently to combine.

Heat the oil in a large heavy-based frying pan to 350°F, or until a cube of bread dropped into the oil browns in 15 seconds. Cook the crab cakes over medium heat for 6 minutes, or until golden brown on both sides. Drain well on crumpled paper towels. Serve the crab cakes with the bowl of avocado salsa and some lime wedges. Garnish with the cilantro leaves.

Garlic Shrimp

🦐 SERVES 4
🦐 PREPARATION TIME: 20 MINUTES
🦐 COOKING TIME: 15 MINUTES

2 lb 12 oz raw shrimp
1/3 cup melted butter
3/4 cup olive oil
8 medium garlic cloves, crushed
2 medium scallions, thinly sliced

Preheat the oven to 500°F. Peel the shrimp, leaving the tails intact. Gently pull out the vein from the back of each shrimp, starting at the head end. Cut a slit down the back of each shrimp.

Combine the butter and oil and divide among four 2-cup ovenproof pots. Divide half the crushed garlic among the pots.

Place the pots on a baking sheet and heat in the oven for 10 minutes, or until the mixture is bubbling. Divide the shrimp and remaining garlic among the pots. Return to the oven for 5 minutes, or until the shrimp are cooked. Stir in the scallions. Season to taste. Serve with bread to mop up the juices.

NOTE: Garlic shrimp can also be made in a cast-iron frying pan in the oven or on the stovetop.

Baked Shrimp with Feta

🦐 SERVES 4
🦐 PREPARATION TIME: 20 MINUTES
🦐 COOKING TIME: 30 MINUTES

10 1/2 oz raw large shrimp
2 tablespoons olive oil
2 small red onions, finely chopped
1 large garlic clove, crushed
1 3/4 cups diced tomatoes
2 tablespoons lemon juice
2 tablespoons fresh oregano or
    1 teaspoon dried
1 1/3 cups feta cheese
extra virgin olive oil, for drizzling
chopped Italian parsley, to garnish

Peel the shrimp, leaving the tails intact. Gently pull out the dark vein from the back of each shrimp, starting at the head end.

Preheat the oven to 350°F. Heat the oil in a saucepan over medium heat, add the onion and cook, stirring, for 3 minutes. Add the garlic and cook for a few seconds, then add the tomato and cook for 10 minutes, or until the mixture has reduced and thickened. Add the lemon juice and oregano. Season to taste.

Pour half the sauce into a 3-cup ovenproof dish, about 6 inches square. Place the shrimp on top, spoon on the sauce and crumble feta over the top. Drizzle with the olive oil and sprinkle with freshly cracked black pepper.

Bake for 15 minutes, or until the shrimp are just cooked. Garnish with the parsley. Serve immediately.

Garlic Shrimp

Lobster with Parsley Mayonnaise

🌿 SERVES 4
🌿 PREPARATION TIME: 25 MINUTES
🌿 COOKING TIME: NIL

2 cooked rock lobsters
mixed lettuce leaves, lemon wedges, and
    snipped chives, to serve

PARSLEY MAYONNAISE
1 cup parsley sprigs, stalks removed, finely
    chopped
3 teaspoons dijon mustard
1 teaspoon honey
1 tablespoon lemon juice
$1/4$ cup) whipping cream
$1/4$ cup mayonnaise

Cut each lobster in half lengthways through the shell. Lift the meat from the tail and body. Crack the legs and prise the meat from them. Remove the cream-colored vein and soft body matter and discard. Cut the lobster meat into $3/4$ inch pieces, cover, and refrigerate.

To make the parsley mayonnaise, put the parsley, mustard, honey, lemon juice, cream, and mayonnaise in a food processor. Blend until combined, then season. Spoon the mixture into a bowl, cover, and refrigerate.

Place a bed of lettuce on each serving plate, top with slices of lobster, and spoon parsley mayonnaise over the top.

Oysters in Potatoes with Cheese Sauce

🌿 SERVES 6–8
🌿 PREPARATION TIME: 15 MINUTES
🌿 COOKING TIME: 25 MINUTES

24 baby new potatoes
vegetable oil, for deep-frying
$1/2$ tablespoon butter
24 fresh oysters
$1/2$ small onion, finely chopped
1 tablespoon brandy
$1/2$ cup whipping cream
$1/4$ cup grated cheddar cheese
2 teaspoons chopped dill

Cook the potatoes in boiling, salted water for 5 minutes, or until tender. Drain and cool. Slice a round from the top of each potato and with a melon baller, scoop a ball from the center of each. Trim the bases to sit flat.

Fill a saucepan one-third full of the oil and heat to 350°F, or until a cube of bread dropped into the oil browns in 15 seconds. Deep-fry the potatoes until golden, then drain on paper towels.

Melt the butter in a saucepan, add the oysters, and toss to seal. Remove from the pan. Add the onion to the pan and fry until soft. Add the brandy and, keeping away from anything flammable, ignite with a match. Allow the flames to die down. Add the cream, bring to a boil, then reduce the heat and simmer until thickened. Remove from the heat, stir in the cheddar and half the dill. Season. Return the oysters to the sauce, then spoon into the potatoes. Broil until golden brown. Sprinkle with the remaining dill.

Lobster with Parsley Mayonnaise

Rosemary Tuna Kebabs

❀ SERVES 4
❀ PREPARATION TIME: 20 MINUTES
❀ COOKING TIME: 20 MINUTES

3 ripe tomatoes
1 tablespoon olive oil
2–3 small red chilies, seeded and chopped
3–4 garlic cloves, crushed
1 red onion, finely chopped
1/4 cup dry white wine
1 lb 5 oz canned chickpeas, drained
3 tablespoons chopped oregano
4 tablespoons chopped Italian parsley
lemon wedges, to serve

TUNA KEBABS
2 lb 4 oz tuna fillet, cut into cubes
8 rosemary stalks, with leaves
olive oil, for brushing

Cut the tomatoes into halves or quarters and scoop out the seeds. Roughly chop the flesh.

Heat the oil in a large non-stick frying pan. Add the chili, garlic, and onion and stir over medium heat for 5 minutes, or until softened. Add the chopped tomato and the white wine. Cook over low heat for 10 minutes, or until the mixture is soft and pulpy and most of the liquid has evaporated.

Stir in the chickpeas with the oregano and parsley. Season to taste.

Heat a broiler or barbecue plate. Thread the tuna onto the rosemary stalks, lightly brush with oil, then cook, turning, for 3 minutes. Do not overcook or the tuna will be dry and fall apart. Serve with the chickpeas and lemon wedges.

Garlic and Ginger Shrimp

🌺 SERVES 4

🌺 PREPARATION TIME: 25 MINUTES

🌺 COOKING TIME: 10 MINUTES

2 lb 4 oz large raw shrimp

2 tablespoons vegetable oil

3–4 garlic cloves, finely chopped

2 inch piece fresh ginger, cut into thin
  matchsticks

2–3 small red chilies, seeded and finely
  chopped

6 cilantro stems, finely chopped

8 scallions, cut diagonally into short
  lengths

½ red pepper, thinly sliced

2 tablespoons lemon juice

½ cup white wine

2 teaspoons grated jaggery or unpacked
  brown sugar

2 teaspoons fish sauce, or to taste

1 tablespoon cilantro leaves, to garnish

Peel the shrimp, leaving the tails intact. Gently cut a slit down the back of each shrimp and remove the dark vein from each. Press each shrimp out flat.

Heat a wok until very hot, add the oil, and swirl to coat the base and side. Stir-fry half of the shrimp, garlic, ginger, chili, and cilantro stem for 1–2 minutes over high heat, or until the shrimp have just turned pink, then remove from the wok and set aside. Repeat with the remaining shrimp, garlic, ginger, chili, and cilantro stem. Remove and set aside.

Add the scallion and pepper to the wok and cook over high heat for 2–3 minutes. Combine the lemon juice, wine, and jaggery, then add to the wok. Boil until the liquid has reduced by two-thirds.

Return the shrimp to the wok and sprinkle with the fish sauce to taste. Toss until the shrimp are heated through. Remove from the heat and serve sprinkled with cilantro.

Clams in Chili Paste

CHILI PASTE
2 tablespoons vegetable oil
2 scallions, sliced
2 garlic cloves, sliced
¼ cup dried shrimp
6 small fresh red chilies, seeded
2 teaspoons grated jaggery or unpacked
    brown sugar
2 teaspoons fish sauce
2 teaspoons tamarind purée

2 lb 4 oz fresh clams
3 garlic cloves, thinly sliced
3 small red chilies, seeded and sliced
    lengthways
1 tablespoon light soy sauce
1 cup fish or chicken stock
1 handful Thai basil
steamed rice, to serve

To make the chili paste, heat the oil in a wok over medium heat and fry the scallion, garlic, dried shrimp, and chili for 3 minutes, or until golden brown. Remove from the wok with a slotted spoon. Reserve the oil in the wok.

Place the shrimp mixture and jaggery in a mortar and pestle or small food processor and pound or process until well blended. Add the fish sauce, tamarind purée, and a pinch of salt, and continue to blend to obtain a finely textured paste.

Soak the clams in cold water for 30 minutes. Discard any broken clams or open ones that don't close when tapped on the bench.

Heat the reserved oil in the wok. Add the garlic, chili, soy sauce, and chili paste. Mix well, then add the stock and bring just to a boil. Add the clams and cook over medium–high heat for 2–3 minutes. Discard any unopened clams. Stir in the basil and serve immediately with steamed rice.

NOTE: Dried shrimp are available from Asian food stores. They are delicious in stir-fries and salads. Store in an airtight container.

Crispy Fried Crab

🌿 SERVES 4
🌿 PREPARATION TIME: 30 MINUTES
🌿 COOKING TIME: 15 MINUTES

2 lb 4 oz fresh crab
1 egg, lightly beaten
1 medium red chili, finely chopped
1/2 teaspoon crushed garlic
1/4 teaspoon ground white pepper
oil, for deep-frying
lemon wedges, to serve

SEASONING MIX
1/3 cup all-purpose flour
1/3 cup rice flour
3 teaspoons sugar
1 teaspoon ground white pepper

Freeze the crab for about 1 hour until immobilized. Scrub the crab clean. Pull back the apron and remove the top shell (it should come off easily and in one piece). Remove the intestines and the gray feathery gills. Twist off the legs and claws. Using a sharp, heavy knife, chop the body into four pieces. Crack the claws with a good hit with the back of a knife.

Beat the egg with the chili, garlic, pepper and 1/2 teaspoon salt in a large bowl. Put the crab pieces in the mixture, cover and refrigerate for 1 hour.

Sift the seasoning ingredients together onto a large plate. Dip all the crab segments in the seasoning and dust off any excess.

Fill a deep-fryer or heavy-based saucepan one-third full of oil and heat to 350°F, or until a cube of bread dropped into the oil browns in 15 seconds. Carefully cook the claws in batches for 7–8 minutes, the body portions for 3–4 minutes, and the legs for 2 minutes. Drain on crumpled paper towels before serving with lemon wedges.

NOTE: Serve the crab as soon as it's cooked. You will need a crab cracker to crack the claws so you can remove the flesh.

Barbecued Octopus

🔥 SERVES 6
🔥 PREPARATION TIME: 15 MINUTES
🔥 COOKING TIME: 5 MINUTES

2/3 cup olive oil
1/3 cup chopped oregano
3 tablespoons chopped Italian parsley
1 tablespoon lemon juice
3 small red chilies, seeded and finely
    chopped
3 medium garlic cloves, crushed
2 lb 4 oz baby octopus
lime wedges, to serve

To make the marinade, combine the oil, herbs, lemon juice, chili and garlic in a large bowl and mix well.

Use a small, sharp knife to remove the octopus heads. Grasp the bodies and push the beaks out from the center with your index finger, then remove and discard. Slit the heads and remove the gut. If the octopus are too large, cut them into smaller portions.

Mix the octopus with the herb marinade. Cover and refrigerate for several hours, or overnight. Drain and reserve the marinade. Cook on a very hot, lightly oiled barbecue or in a very hot frying pan for 3–5 minutes, or until the flesh turns white. Turn frequently and brush generously with the marinade during cooking.

Grilled Squid

🔥 SERVES 6
🔥 PREPARATION TIME: 10 MINUTES
🔥 COOKING TIME: 10 MINUTES

2 lb 4 oz squid
1 cup olive oil
2 tablespoons lemon juice
2 garlic cloves, crushed
2 tablespoons chopped oregano
2 tablespoons chopped Italian parsley,
    to serve
6 lemon wedges, to serve

To clean the squid, gently pull the tentacles away from the tube (the intestines should come away at the same time). Remove the intestines from the tentacles by cutting under the eyes, then remove the beak if it remains in the center of the tentacles by using your fingers to push up the center. Pull away the quill from inside the body and remove. Remove and discard any white membrane. Under cold running water, pull away the skin from the hood. Cut the hood into 1/2 inch rings and place in the bowl with the tentacles. Add the oil, lemon juice, garlic, and oregano to the bowl, and toss to coat the squid. Leave to marinate for 30 minutes.

Heat a barbecue or chargrill pan until hot. Drain the squid rings and cook them in batches for 1–2 minutes on each side.

Season the squid rings and sprinkle with the parsley. Serve with lemon wedges.

Rosemary Tuna Kebabs

Stuffed Shrimp Omelets

🌼 MAKES: 8

🌼 PREPARATION TIME: 25 MINUTES

🌼 COOKING TIME: 15 MINUTES

1 lb 2 oz raw shrimp
1½ tablespoons oil
4 eggs, lightly beaten
2 tablespoons fish sauce
8 medium scallions, chopped
6 medium cilantro stems, chopped
2 medium garlic cloves, chopped
1 small red chili, seeded and chopped
2 teaspoons lime juice
2 teaspoons grated jaggery
   or unpacked brown sugar
3 tablespoons chopped cilantro leaves
1 small red chili, extra, chopped
   to garnish
cilantro sprigs, to garnish
sweet chili sauce, to serve

Peel the shrimp. Gently pull out the dark vein from the back of each shrimp, starting from the head end, then chop the shrimp meat.

Heat a wok over high heat, add 2 teaspoons of the oil and swirl to coat. Combine the egg with half of the fish sauce. Add 2 tablespoons of the mixture to the wok and swirl to a 6¼ inch round. Cook for 1 minute, then gently lift out. Repeat with the remaining egg mixture to make eight omelets.

Heat the remaining oil in the wok. Add the shrimp, scallions, cilantro stem, garlic and chili. Stir-fry for 3–4 minutes, or until the shrimp are cooked. Stir in the lime juice, jaggery, cilantro leaves and the remaining fish sauce.

Divide the shrimp mixture among the omelets and fold each into a small firm parcel. Cut a slit in the top and garnish with the chili and cilantro sprigs. Serve with sweet chili sauce.

Seafood Quenelles

PREPARATION TIME: 30 MINUTES
COOKING TIME: 40 MINUTES

QUENELLES
7 oz skinless firm white fish fillets
5½ oz scallops
5½ oz raw shrimp meat
1 egg white
1 teaspoon finely grated lemon zest
½ cup whipping cream
3 tablespoons finely snipped chives

TOMATO COULIS
1 tablespoon olive oil
1 garlic clove, crushed
1¾ cups canned crushed tomatoes
⅔ cup fish stock or water
2 tablespoons whipping cream
2 tablespoons snipped chives
4 cups fish stock

To make the quenelles, pat the fish, scallops, and shrimp meat dry with paper towels. Roughly mince the fish in a food processor for 30 seconds, then remove. Process the scallops and shrimp meat, then return the fish to the processor, add the egg white and lemon zest, and process for about 30 seconds, or until finely minced. With the motor running, slowly pour in the cream until the mixture just thickens — do not overprocess. Stir in the chives, then transfer to a bowl. Cover and refrigerate for at least 3 hours.

Using two wet tablespoons, mold 2 tablespoons of mixture at a time into egg shapes. Place on a baking sheet lined with parchment paper. Cover and refrigerate for 30 minutes.

To make the tomato coulis, heat the oil in a saucepan, add the garlic, and stir over medium heat for about 30 seconds. Add the tomatoes, stock or water, and season. Simmer for 30 minutes, stirring occasionally, until thickened and reduced.

Push the tomato mixture through a fine sieve, discard the pulp, and return the liquid to the cleaned pan. Add the cream and chives and reheat gently, stirring.

In a large frying pan, heat the fish stock until just simmering, but be careful not to boil the stock. Gently lower the quenelles into the poaching liquid in batches, then cover the pan, reduce the heat, and poach each batch for about 5–6 minutes, or until cooked through. Lift out using a slotted spoon and drain on crumpled paper towels.

Spoon some of the tomato coulis onto each serving plate and top with the seafood quenelles.

Coconut Shrimp with Chili Dressing

24 large raw shrimp

all-purpose flour, to coat

1 egg

1 tablespoon milk

1 cup shredded coconut

1 handful cilantro leaves, chopped, plus
    extra, to garnish

2½ tablespoons vegetable oil

2¾ cups red Asian shallots, chopped

2 garlic cloves, finely chopped

2 teaspoons finely chopped fresh ginger

1 red chili, seeded and thinly sliced

1 teaspoon ground turmeric

9½ fl oz canned coconut cream

2 kaffir lime leaves, thinly sliced

2 teaspoons lime juice

2 teaspoons grated jaggery or unpacked
    brown sugar

3 teaspoons fish sauce

vegetable oil, for deep-frying

Peel the shrimp and gently pull out the dark vein from each shrimp back, starting from the head end. Holding the shrimp by their tails, coat them in flour, then dip them into the combined egg and milk, and then in the combined coconut and cilantro. Refrigerate for 30 minutes.

To make the chili dressing, heat the oil in a saucepan and cook the shallots, garlic, ginger, chili, and turmeric over medium heat for 3–5 minutes, or until fragrant. Add the coconut cream, makrut leaves, lime juice, jaggery, and fish sauce. Bring to a boil, then reduce the heat and simmer for 2–3 minutes, or until thick. Keep warm.

Fill a wok or deep heavy-based saucepan one-third full of oil and heat to 350°F, or until a cube of bread dropped into the oil browns in 15 seconds. Holding the shrimp by their tails, gently lower them into the wok and cook in batches for 3–5 minutes, or until golden. Drain on crumpled paper towels and season with salt.

Add the extra cilantro to the chili dressing and serve with the shrimp.

Stuffed Sardines

✻ SERVES 4–6
✻ PREPARATION TIME: 20 MINUTES
✻ COOKING TIME: 25 MINUTES

2 lb 4 oz butterflied fresh sardines
¼ cup olive oil
½ cup fresh white breadcrumbs
¼ cup golden raisins
¼ cup pine nuts, toasted
¾ oz canned anchovy fillets, drained and
    mashed
1 tablespoon finely chopped Italian parsley
2 scallions, finely chopped

Preheat the oven to 400°F. Grease a baking dish. Open out each sardine and place, skin side down, on a chopping board.

Heat half the oil in a frying pan. Add the breadcrumbs and cook over medium heat, stirring until light golden. Drain on paper towels.

Put half the fried breadcrumbs in a bowl and stir in the golden raisins, pine nuts, anchovies, parsley, and scallion. Season to taste. Spoon about 2 teaspoons of the mixture into each prepared sardine, then carefully fold up to enclose the stuffing.

Place the stuffed sardines in a single layer in the baking dish. Sprinkle any remaining stuffing over the top of the sardines, along with the cooked breadcrumbs. Drizzle with the remaining olive oil and bake for 15–20 minutes.

Clams in White Wine

2 lb 4 oz clams (see Note)
2 large tomatoes
2 tablespoons olive oil
1 small onion, finely chopped
2 medium garlic cloves, crushed
1 tablespoon chopped Italian parsley
pinch freshly grated nutmeg
1/3 cup dry white wine
Italian parsley, to garnish

Soak the clams in salted water for 1 hour to release any grit. Rinse under running water and discard any open clams. Score a cross in the base of each tomato. Put in a heatproof bowl and cover with boiling water. Leave for 30 seconds, then transfer to cold water and peel the skin away from the cross. Cut the tomatoes in half, scoop out the seeds and finely chop.

Heat the oil in a large flameproof casserole dish and cook the onion over low heat for 5 minutes, or until softened. Add the garlic and tomato and cook for 5 minutes. Stir in the parsley and nutmeg and season. Add 1/3 cup water.

Add the clams and cook over low heat until they open. Discard any clams that don't open. Add the wine and cook over low heat for 3–4 minutes, or until the sauce thickens, gently moving the dish back and forth a few times, rather than stirring the clams, so that the clams stay in the shells. Serve at once, with bread.

NOTE: You can use mussels instead of clams in this recipe.

Creamy Baked Scallops

PREPARATION TIME: 20 MINUTES

COOKING TIME: 10 MINUTES

24 scallops, on the shell
1 cup fish stock
1 cup dry white wine
1/4 cup butter
4 medium scallions, chopped
1 medium bacon slice, finely chopped
1 cup thinly sliced white mushrooms
1/4 cup all-purpose flour
3/4 cup whipping cream
1 teaspoon lemon juice
1 cup fresh breadcrumbs
2 tablespoons melted butter, extra

Take the scallops off their shells. Rinse and reserve the shells. If the scallops need to be cut off, use a small, sharp knife to slice them free, being careful to leave as little meat on the shell as possible. Slice or pull off any vein, membrane or hard white muscle, leaving any roe attached. Cut the scallops in half.

Heat the fish stock and white wine in a saucepan and add the scallops. Cover and simmer over medium heat for 2–3 minutes, or until the scallops are opaque and tender. Remove the scallops with a slotted spoon, cover and set aside. Bring the liquid in the pan to a boil and reduce until 1 1/2 cups remain.

Melt the butter in a saucepan and add the scallions, bacon and mushrooms. Cook over medium heat for 3 minutes, stirring occasionally, until the scallions are soft but not brown.

Stir in the flour and cook for 2 minutes. Remove from the heat and gradually stir in the reduced stock. Return to the heat and stir until the mixture boils and thickens. Reduce the heat and simmer for 2 minutes. Stir in the cream, lemon juice and season to taste. Cover, set aside and keep warm.

Combine the breadcrumbs and extra butter in a small bowl. Preheat the broiler to high.

Divide the scallops among the shells. Spoon the warm sauce over the scallops and sprinkle with the breadcrumb mixture. Place under the broiler until the breadcrumbs are golden brown. Serve immediately.

Shrimp Cocktail

¼ cup whole-egg mayonnaise
2 teaspoons ketchup
dash of Tabasco sauce
¼ teaspoon worcestershire sauce
2 teaspoons heavy cream
¼ teaspoon lemon juice
24 cooked large shrimp
4 lettuce leaves, shredded
lemon wedges, for serving

Mix the mayonnaise, ketchup, Tabasco sauce, cream and juice together in a small bowl.

Peel the shrimp, leaving the tails intact on eight of them. Gently pull out the dark vein from the back of each shrimp, starting at the head end.

Divide the lettuce among four glasses. Arrange the shrimp without the tails in the glasses and drizzle with the sauce. Hang two of the remaining shrimp over the edge of each glass and serve with lemon wedges.

Salt Cod Purée (Brandade de Morue)

½ salt cod
1¼ cups diced roasting potatoes
¾ cup olive oil
1 cup whole milk
4 medium garlic cloves, crushed
2 tablespoons lemon juice
olive oil, extra, to drizzle

Put the salt cod in a large bowl, cover with cold water and soak for 24 hours, changing the water frequently. Drain the cod and place in a large saucepan of clean water. Bring to a boil over medium heat, reduce the heat and simmer for 30 minutes. Drain, then cool for 15 minutes.

Meanwhile, cook the potatoes in a saucepan of boiling salted water for 12–15 minutes, or until tender. Drain and keep warm.

Remove the skin from the fish and break the flesh into large flaky pieces, discarding any bones. Put the flesh in a food processor. Using two separate pans, gently warm the oil in one, and the milk and garlic in another.

Start the food processor and, with the motor running, alternately add small amounts of the milk and oil until you have a thick, paste-like mixture. Add the potato and process this in short bursts until combined, being careful not to overwork the mixture once the potato has been added. Transfer to a bowl and gradually add the lemon juice, to taste, and plenty of freshly ground black pepper. Gently lighten the mixture by fluffing it up with a fork. Drizzle with the oil before serving. Serve warm or cold with fried bread.

Shrimp Cocktails

Stuffed Crab

⚘ SERVES 4

⚘ PREPARATION TIME: 30 MINUTES

⚘ COOKING TIME: 50 MINUTES

4 live crabs (about 1 lb 10 oz each)
   (see Note)
¼ cup salt
⅓ cup olive oil
1 onion, finely chopped
1 garlic clove
½ cup dry white wine
1 cup puréed tomatoes
¼ teaspoon finely chopped tarragon
2 tablespoons dry breadcrumbs
2 tablespoons chopped Italian parsley
2 tablespoons butter, chopped

Put the crabs in the freezer for 1 hour to immobilize them. Bring a large saucepan of water to a boil. Add the salt and the crabs. Return to a boil and simmer, uncovered, for 15 minutes. Remove the crabs from the water and cool for 30 minutes. Extract the meat from the legs. Lift the apron – the small flap on the underside of the crab – and prise off the top hard shell, without destroying the top shell, which is needed for serving. Reserve any liquid in a bowl. Remove the soft internal organs and pull off the grey feathery gills. Take out the meat and chop finely with the leg meat. Scoop out all the brown paste from the shells and mix with the chopped meat.

Heat the oil in a frying pan and cook the onion and garlic for 5–6 minutes, or until softened. Stir in the wine and puréed tomatoes. Simmer for 3–4 minutes, then add any reserved crab liquid. Simmer for 3–4 minutes. Add the crabmeat and tarragon, then season. Simmer for about 5 minutes, or until thick. Discard the garlic.

Preheat the oven to 425°F. Rinse out and dry the crab shells. Divide the crab mixture among them, levelling the surface. Combine the breadcrumbs and parsley and sprinkle over the top. Dot with the butter. Bake for 6–8 minutes, until the butter melts and the breadcrumbs brown. Serve hot.

NOTE: The crab traditionally used in this recipe is the centollo, or spider crab. Substitute any large-bodied fresh crab, but avoid swimmer or spanner crabs, which do not have enough flesh in them.

Mussels with Black Beans and Cilantro

🌺 SERVES 4

🌺 PREPARATION TIME: 20 MINUTES

🌺 COOKING TIME: 10 MINUTES

3 lb 5 oz black mussels

1 tablespoon peanut oil

2 tablespoons black beans, rinsed and mashed

2 medium garlic cloves, finely chopped

1 teaspoon finely chopped fresh ginger

2 long red chilies, seeded and finely chopped

2 teaspoons finely chopped cilantro leaves

1 tablespoon finely chopped cilantro stem

1/4 cup Chinese rice wine

2 tablespoons lime juice

2 teaspoons sugar

steamed rice, to serve

Scrub the mussels with a stiff brush and pull out the hairy beards. Discard any broken mussels, or open ones that don't close when tapped on the bench. Rinse well.

Heat a wok until very hot, add the oil and swirl to coat the base and side. Add the black beans, garlic, ginger, chili, 1 teaspoon cilantro leaves and the cilantro stem, and cook over low heat for 2–3 minutes, or until fragrant. Pour in the rice wine and increase the heat to high. Add half the mussels in a single layer and cover with a tight-fitting lid. Cook for 2–3 minutes, or until the mussels have just opened. Discard any mussels that do not open. Remove from the wok, and repeat with the remaining mussels until all are cooked.

Transfer the mussels to a serving dish, leaving the cooking liquid in the wok. Add the lime juice, sugar and remaining cilantro leaves to the wok and cook for 30 seconds. Pour the sauce over the mussels and serve with steamed rice.

California Rolls

- SERVES 12
- PREPARATION TIME: 25 MINUTES + 1 HOUR DRAINING + COOLING
- COOKING TIME: 25 MINUTES

1 cup Japanese short-grain rice
1 tablespoon rice vinegar
2 generous pinches of sugar
1 large egg
1 teaspoon sake
1 teaspoon oil
2 sheets roasted nori, 8 x 7 inches
2 x 1 1/4 oz crabsticks, cut into strips
1/4 cup pickled daikon, cut into very thin batons
1/4 cup carrot, cut into very thin batons
1/4 cup cucumber, cut into very thin batons
Japanese soy sauce, to serve
wasabi paste, to serve
pickled ginger, to serve

Wash the rice under cold running water until the water runs clear, then drain thoroughly. Drain for an hour. Put the rice into a saucepan and cover with cold water. Cover the pan and bring the water to a boil. Reduce the heat and simmer for 10 minutes. When the rice is cooked, remove the pan from the heat and leave, covered, for 10 minutes.

To make the sushi dressing, mix together the vinegar, a pinch of the sugar and a pinch of salt.

Spread the rice over the base of a non-metallic dish or bowl, pour the sushi dressing over the top and use a rice paddle or spatula to mix the dressing through the rice, separating the grains as you do so. Fan the rice until it cools to room temperature. Cover the pan with a damp dish towel and set aside — do not refrigerate.

To make the omelet, gently combine the egg, sake, a pinch of sugar and a pinch of salt. Heat the oil in a small frying pan. Add the egg mixture and cook until firm around the edges but still slightly soft in the middle. Roll the omelet, then tip it out of the pan. Cool, then slice into strips.

Put a nori sheet on a sushi mat, shiny side down. Add half of the rice, leaving a 3/4 inch gap at the edge furthest away from you. Lay half of the fillings on the rice in the following order: omelet, crabstick, daikon, carrot, cucumber. Starting with the end nearest to you, tightly roll the mat and the nori. Repeat this process with the remaining ingredients.

Using a sharp knife, cut each roll into six slices. After cutting each slice, rinse the knife under cold running water to prevent sticking. Serve with Japanese soy sauce, wasabi and pickled ginger.

Seafood Terrine

🌭 SERVES 8

🌭 PREPARATION TIME: 1 HOUR

🌭 COOKING TIME: 40 MINUTES

FIRST LAYER

1 lb 2 oz raw shrimp, chilled

2 egg whites, chilled

pinch freshly grated nutmeg

1 cup whipping cream, chilled

5$\frac{1}{2}$ oz baby green beans, trimmed

SECOND LAYER

9 oz skinless salmon or ocean trout fillet,
   chopped

2 egg whites, chilled

2 tablespoons snipped chives

1 cup whipping cream, chilled

TOMATO COULIS

1 lb 10 oz very ripe plum tomatoes

2 tablespoons extra virgin olive oil

1 onion, very finely chopped

2 tablespoons Grand Marnier (optional)

trimmed watercress, to garnish

Preheat the oven to 350°F. Brush a 6-cup bar pan, measuring 4$\frac{1}{2}$ x 8$\frac{1}{2}$ inches, with oil and line the base with parchment paper.

To make the first layer, peel the shrimp and gently pull out the dark vein from each shrimp back, starting at the head end. Finely chop the shrimp in a food processor. Add the egg whites one at a time, processing until smooth. Season. Gradually add the cream. Don't overprocess or it may curdle. Spoon into the prepared bar pan, cover, and refrigerate. Cook the beans in boiling water for 3 minutes, or until just tender, then drain and plunge into cold water. Drain and dry with paper towels. Arrange lengthways over the shrimp mixture.

To make the second layer, process the fish in a food processor until finely chopped. Add the egg whites one at a time and process until smooth. Add the chives. Gradually pour in the cream. Do not overprocess or it may curdle. Spread evenly over the beans.

Cover the terrine tightly with foil brushed with oil and put in a baking sheet. Pour cold water into the sheet to come halfway up the side of the pan. Bake for 35 minutes, or until lightly set in the center. Cool before removing the foil. Cover with plastic wrap and refrigerate until firm. Serve at room temperature.

Meanwhile, to make the tomato coulis, score a cross in the base of each tomato. Put in a heatproof bowl and cover with boiling water. Leave for 30 seconds, then transfer to cold water, drain and peel away the skin from the cross. Cut the tomatoes in half, scoop out the seeds, and chop the flesh. Heat the oil in a saucepan, add the onion and stir for 2–3 minutes, or until tender. Add the tomato and cook over medium heat, stirring often, for 8 minutes, or until reduced and thickened. Stir in the Grand Marnier and cook for 1 minute. Cool, then process in a food processor until smooth. Season and serve with slices of terrine, garnished with watercress.

Marinated Salmon Strips

🌺 SERVES 4
🌺 PREPARATION TIME: 15 MINUTES +
🌺 COOKING TIME: NIL

2 sashimi-grade salmon fillets, each about
    14 oz, skinned
1 1/2 inch piece fresh ginger, grated
1 garlic clove, finely chopped
3 scallions, finely chopped
1 teaspoon sugar
2 tablespoons Japanese soy sauce
1/2 cup sake
pickled ginger, to garnish
pickled cucumber, to garnish

Cut the salmon into thin strips and arrange them in a single layer in a large deep dish.

Put the ginger, garlic, scallion, sugar, 1 teaspoon salt, soy sauce, and sake in a small bowl and stir to combine. Pour the marinade over the salmon, cover, and refrigerate for 1 hour.

Arrange the salmon, strip by strip, on a serving plate. Garnish with the pickled ginger and cucumber, and serve chilled.

Shrimp Croustade

🌺 SERVES 6
🌺 PREPARATION TIME: 45 MINUTES
🌺 COOKING TIME: 25 MINUTES

1/2 loaf unsliced white bread, crust
    removed
1/2 cup olive oil
1 garlic clove, crushed

FILLING
1 lb 2 oz raw shrimp
1 1/2 cups fish stock
2 slices lemon
1/4 cup butter
6 scallions, chopped
1 oz all-purpose flour
1 tablespoon lemon juice
1 teaspoon chopped dill
1/4 cup whipping cream

Preheat the oven to 425°F. Cut the bread into slices 2 inches thick. Cut each slice diagonally to form triangles. Cut another triangle 1/2 inch inside each piece, then scoop out the centers to create cavities for the filling, leaving a base on each. Heat the oil and garlic in a frying pan, brush all over the bread cases, then bake for about 10 minutes, or until golden.

To make the filling, peel the shrimp and pull out the dark vein from each shrimp back, starting at the head end. Chop the shrimp, put in a saucepan, and cover with the stock. Add the lemon, simmer for 15 minutes, strain and reserve the liquid and ahrimp separately. Melt the butter in a saucepan, add the scallion and stir until soft. Stir in the flour and cook for 2 minutes. Add in the reserved shrimp liquid and stir for 5 minutes, or until the sauce thickens. Add the lemon juice, dill, cream, and shrimp, and stir until heated through. To serve, spoon the filling into the warm bread cases.

Marinated Salmon Strips

Squid with Green Peppercorns

🌺 SERVES 4

🌺 PREPARATION TIME: 10 MINUTES

🌺 COOKING TIME: 5 MINUTES

1 lb 5 oz squid tubes, washed and dried

2 teaspoons chopped cilantro stem

3 garlic cloves, crushed

1/3 cup vegetable oil

1 oz Thai green peppercorns on the stalk,
    in brine, or lightly crushed fresh
    peppercorns

2 tablespoons Thai mushroom soy sauce

1/2 teaspoon grated jaggery or unpacked
    brown sugar

1 large handful Thai basil

Cut the squid tubes in half lengthways. Clean and remove the quills. Score a diamond pattern on the inside of the squid. Cut into 1 1/2 inch square pieces.

Put the cilantro stem, 1 garlic clove, and 1 tablespoon of the oil in a food processor and process to form a smooth paste. Mix together the paste and squid pieces, cover, and marinate in the refrigerator for 30 minutes.

Heat a wok over high heat, add the remaining oil, and swirl to coat. Add the squid pieces and the remaining garlic and stir-fry for 1 minute. Add the peppercorns and stir-fry for a further 2 minutes, or until the squid is just cooked — it will toughen if overcooked. Add the soy sauce and jaggery, and stir until the sugar has dissolved. Serve immediately, garnished with Thai basil.

Asian Oysters

※ SERVES 4
※ PREPARATION TIME: 15 MINUTES
※ COOKING TIME: 5 MINUTES

12 oysters, on the shell
2 medium garlic cloves, finely chopped
¾ x ¾ inch piece ginger, cut into thin batons
2 medium scallions, thinly sliced, diagonally
¼ cup Japanese soy sauce
¼ cup peanut oil
cilantro leaves, to garnish

Line a large bamboo steamer with parchment paper. Arrange the oysters in a single layer on top.

Put the garlic, ginger and scallions in a bowl, mix together well, then sprinkle over the oysters. Spoon 1 teaspoon of soy sauce over each oyster. Cover and steam over a wok of simmering water for 2 minutes.

Heat the peanut oil in a small saucepan until smoking and carefully drizzle a little over each oyster. Garnish with the cilantro leaves and serve immediately.

Scallop Ceviche

※ SERVES 2–4
※ PREPARATION TIME: 20 MINUTES
※ COOKING TIME: NIL

16 scallops, on the shell
1 teaspoon finely grated lime zest
2 medium garlic cloves, chopped
2 medium red chilies, seeded and chopped
¼ cup lime juice
1 tablespoon chopped Italian parsley
1 tablespoon olive oil

Take the scallops off their shells. Rinse and reserve the shells. If the scallops need to be cut off, use a small, sharp knife to slice them free, being careful to leave as little meat on the shell as possible. Slice or pull off any vein, membrane or hard white muscle, leaving any roe attached.

In a non-metallic bowl, mix together the lime zest, garlic, chili, lime juice, parsley and olive oil, and season. Put the scallops in the dressing and stir to coat. Cover with plastic wrap and refrigerate for 2 hours to "cook" the scallop meat.

To serve, slide each scallop back onto a half shell and spoon the dressing over. Serve cold.

NOTE: The scallops will keep for 2 days in the dressing.

Asian Oysters

Moules Marinière

☘ SERVES 4
☘ PREPARATION TIME: 15 MINUTES
☘ COOKING TIME: 35 MINUTES

24 black mussels
1 celery stalk, chopped
1 cup dry white wine
3 onions, chopped
1½ cups fish stock
4 Italian parsley sprigs
1 thyme sprig
1 bay leaf
¼ cup butter
2 garlic cloves, crushed
1 teaspoon all-purpose flour
dill sprigs, to garnish

Scrub the mussels with a stiff brush and pull out the hairy beards. Discard any broken mussels, or open ones that don't close when tapped on the bench. Rinse well.

Put the mussels, celery, wine, and one-third of the onion in a large saucepan and bring rapidly to a boil. Cover and cook, shaking the pan frequently, for 4–5 minutes, discarding any unopened mussels after that time.

Pull off and discard the empty side of each shell. Set aside the mussels in the shells, cover, and keep warm.

Strain and reserve the cooking liquid, discarding the vegetables.

In a saucepan, heat the fish stock, parsley, thyme, and bay leaf. Bring to a boil, then reduce the heat, cover and simmer for 10 minutes. Remove the herbs.

Melt the butter in a large saucepan, add the garlic and remaining onion, and stir over low heat for 5–10 minutes, or until the onion is soft but not brown. Stir in the flour and cook for 1 minute, or until pale and foaming. Remove from the heat and gradually stir in the reserved mussel liquid and fish stock. Return to the heat and stir until the mixture boils and thickens. Reduce the heat and simmer, uncovered, for about 10 minutes.

Divide the reserved mussels among four soup bowls. Ladle the liquid over the mussels and garnish with the dill sprigs. Serve immediately with slices of crusty bread.

Scallops Provençale

🌸 SERVES 4
🌸 PREPARATION TIME: 20 MINUTES
🌸 COOKING TIME: 30 MINUTES

20 scallops, on the shell
3 cups medium tomatoes
¼ cup olive oil
1 medium onion, finely chopped
4 medium French shallots, finely chopped
¼ cup dry white wine
¼ cup butter
4 medium garlic cloves, crushed
2 tablespoons finely chopped Italian
    parsley
½ teaspoon thyme
2 tablespoons fresh breadcrumbs

Take the scallops off their shells. Rinse and reserve the shells. If the scallops need to be cut off, use a small, sharp knife to slice them free, being careful to leave as little meat on the shell as possible. Slice or pull off any vein, membrane or hard white muscle, leaving any roe attached.

Score a cross in the base of each tomato. Put the tomatoes in a heatproof bowl and cover with boiling water. Leave for 30 seconds, then transfer to cold water and peel the skin away from the cross. Cut each tomato in half, scoop out the seeds and finely dice the flesh.

Heat 2 tablespoons of the oil in a frying pan over medium heat until hot, add the onion and shallots, then reduce the heat to low and cook slowly for 5 minutes, or until soft. Add the wine and simmer for several minutes until reduced slightly, then add the tomato. Season and cook, stirring occasionally, for 20 minutes, or until thick and pulpy. Preheat the oven to 350°F.

Heat the butter and remaining oil in a frying pan over high heat until foamy. Cook half the scallops for 1–2 minutes each side, or until lightly golden. Remove and repeat with the remaining scallops. Set aside.

Add the garlic to the hot scallop pan and stir for 1 minute. Remove from the heat and stir in the parsley, thyme and breadcrumbs.

To serve, warm the shells on a baking sheet in the oven. Put a small amount of tomato mixture on each shell, top with a scallop and sprinkle with the breadcrumb and parsley mixture.

meat and poultry

Carpaccio

🔥 SERVES 8
🔥 PREPARATION TIME: 15 MINUTES
🔥 COOKING TIME: NIL

14 oz beef tenderloin
1 tablespoon extra virgin olive oil
arugula leaves, torn, to serve
2/3 cup shaved parmesan cheese, to serve
medium black olives, cut into slivers,
    to serve

Remove all the visible fat and sinew from the beef, then freeze for 1–2 hours, until firm but not solid. This makes the meat easier to slice thinly.

Cut paper-thin slices of beef with a large, sharp knife. Arrange on a serving platter and allow to return to room temperature.

Just before serving, drizzle with oil, then scatter with arugula, parmesan and olives.

NOTE: The beef can be cut into slices a few hours in advance, covered and refrigerated. Drizzle with oil and garnish with the other ingredients just before serving.

Quail in Grape Leaves

☙ SERVES 4

☙ PREPARATION TIME: 15 MINUTES

☙ COOKING TIME: 25 MINUTES

12 medium black grapes, halved
1 tablespoon olive oil
1 medium garlic clove, crushed
4 large quail
8 fresh or preserved grape leaves
4 medium prosciutto slices
black grapes, extra, halved, to garnish

Preheat the oven to 350°F. Toss the grapes with the oil and crushed garlic. Put six grape halves in the cavity of each quail.

If you are using fresh vine leaves, blanch them for 1 minute in boiling water, then remove the central stem. If using preserved vine leaves, wash them under running water to remove any excess preserving liquid.

Wrap each quail in a piece of prosciutto and place each quail on top of a vine leaf. Place another vine leaf on top of each quail and wrap into parcels, tying with string to secure. Bake on a baking sheet for 20–25 minutes, or until juices run clear when tested with a skewer. Serve garnished with the extra grapes.

Sweet and Sour Liver (Fegato Garbo e Dolce)

☙ SERVES 4

☙ PREPARATION TIME: 10 MINUTES

☙ COOKING TIME: 10 MINUTES

3 tablespoons butter
1/3 cup olive oil
1 lb 5 oz calves' livers, cut into
    long thin slices
1 cup fresh white breadcrumbs
1 tablespoon sugar
2 medium garlic cloves, crushed
1/4 cup red wine vinegar
1 tablespoon chopped Italian parsley

Heat the butter and half the oil in a heavy-based frying pan over medium heat. Coat the liver in breadcrumbs, pressing them on firmly with your hands. Shake off the excess and place in the pan when the butter begins to foam. Cook on each side for 1 minute, or until the crust is brown and crisp. Remove from the pan and keep warm.

Add the remaining oil to the frying pan and cook the sugar and garlic over low heat until golden. Add the vinegar and cook for 30 seconds, or until almost evaporated. Add the parsley and pour over the liver. Serve hot or at room temperature.

Quail in Vine Leaves

Chicken Ballottine

🌠 SERVES 8

🌠 PREPARATION TIME: 40 MINUTES

🌠 COOKING TIME: 1 HOUR 45 MINUTES

3 lb 8 oz chicken
2 red peppers
2 lb 4 oz Swiss chard
1 1/2 tablespoons butter
1 onion, finely chopped
1 garlic clove, crushed
1/2 cup grated parmesan cheese
1 cup fresh breadcrumbs
1 tablespoon chopped oregano
3/4 cup ricotta cheese

To bone the chicken, cut through the skin on the center back with a sharp knife. Separate the flesh from the bone down one side to the breast, being careful not to pierce the skin. Follow along the bones closely with the knife, gradually easing the meat from the thigh, drumstick and wing. Cut through the thigh bone where it meets the drumstick and cut off the wing tip. Repeat on the other side, then lift the rib cage away, leaving the flesh in one piece and the drumsticks still attached to the flesh. Scrape all the meat from the drumstick and wings, discarding the bones. Turn the wing and drumstick flesh inside the chicken and lay the chicken out flat, skin side down. Refrigerate.

Preheat the oven to 350°F. Cut the peppers into large flattish pieces, discarding the membranes and seeds. Cook, skin side up, under a hot broiler until the skin blisters and blackens. Cool in a plastic bag, then peel.

Discard the stalks from the Swiss chard and finely shred the leaves. Melt the butter in a large frying pan and cook the onion and garlic over medium heat for 5 minutes, or until soft. Add the Swiss chard and stir until wilted and all the moisture has evaporated. Cool. In a food processor, process the Swiss chard and onion mixture with the parmesan, breadcrumbs, oregano, and half the ricotta. Season with salt and pepper.

Spread the Swiss chard mixture over the chicken and lay the pepper pieces over the top. Form the remaining ricotta into a roll and place across the width of the chicken. Fold the sides of the chicken in and over the filling so they overlap slightly. Tuck the ends in neatly. Secure with toothpicks, then tie with string at 1 1/4 inch intervals.

Grease a piece of foil and place the chicken in the center. Roll the chicken up in the foil. Bake on a baking sheet for 1 1/4 hours, or until the juices run clear when a skewer is inserted in the center. Cool, then refrigerate until cold before removing the foil, toothpicks, and string. Cut into 1/2 inch slices to serve.

Chicken Liver and Grand Marnier Pâté

※ SERVES 8
※ PREPARATION TIME: 20 MINUTES
※ COOKING TIME: 10 MINUTES

1 lb 10 oz chicken livers, well trimmed
1 cup milk
3/4 cup butter, softened
4 scallions, finely chopped
1 tablespoon Grand Marnier
1 tablespoon frozen orange juice
    concentrate, thawed
1/2 orange, very thinly sliced

JELLIED LAYER
1 tablespoon orange juice concentrate
1 tablespoon Grand Marnier
1 1/4 cups canned chicken consommé,
    undiluted
2 1/2 teaspoons powdered gelatine

Put the chicken livers in a bowl, add the milk and stir to combine. Cover and refrigerate for 1 hour. Drain the livers and discard the milk. Rinse in cold water, drain, and pat dry with paper towels.

Melt one-third of the butter in a frying pan, add the scallion, and cook for 2–3 minutes, or until tender, but not brown. Add the livers and cook, stirring, over medium heat for 4–5 minutes, or until just cooked. Remove from the heat and cool a little.

Transfer the livers to a food processor and process until very smooth. Chop the remaining butter, add to the processor with the Grand Marnier and orange juice concentrate and process until creamy. Season, to taste, with salt and freshly ground black pepper. Transfer to a 5-cup capacity serving dish, cover the surface with plastic wrap, and chill for 1 1/2 hours, or until firm.

For the jellied layer, whisk together the orange juice concentrate, Grand Marnier and 1/2 cup of the consommé in a jug. Sprinkle the gelatine over the liquid in an even layer and leave until the gelatine is spongy – do not stir. Heat the remaining consommé in a pan, remove from the heat, and add the gelatine mixture. Stir to dissolve the gelatine, then leave to cool and thicken to the consistency of uncooked egg white, but not set.

Press the orange slices lightly into the surface of the pâté and spoon the thickened jelly evenly over the top. Refrigerate until set. Serve at room temperature with toast or crackers.

NOTE: Grand Marnier is a cognac-based liqueur with an orange flavor.

Teppan Yaki

❀ SERVES 4
❀ PREPARATION TIME: 45 MINUTES
❀ COOKING TIME: 25 MINUTES

12 oz steak fillets, partially frozen, thinly
    sliced
4 small slender eggplants
3½ oz fresh shiitake mushrooms
3½ oz small green beans, trimmed
6 pattypan squash
1 red or green pepper, seeded and
    membrane removed
6 scallions
¾ cup drained canned bamboo shoots
¼ cup vegetable oil
steamed rice, to serve

Place the meat slices in a single layer on a large serving platter, season well, and set aside. Trim the ends from the eggplants and cut the flesh into long, very thin diagonal slices. Trim any hard stems from the mushrooms. Top and tail the beans. If the beans are longer than about 2¾ inches, cut them in half. Quarter, halve, or leave the squash whole, depending on the size. Cut the pepper into thin strips and slice the scallions into lengths about 2¾ inches long, discarding the tops. Arrange all the vegetables (including the bamboo shoots) in separate bundles on a plate.

When the diners are seated, heat an electric grill or electric frying pan until very hot and then lightly brush it with the oil. Quickly fry about a quarter of the meat, searing on both sides, and then push it over to the edge of the pan. Add about a quarter of the vegetables and quickly stir-fry, adding a little more oil as needed. Serve a small portion of the meat and vegetables to the diners, who dip the food into a sauce of their choice. Repeat the process with the remaining meat and vegetables, cooking in batches as extra helpings are required. Serve with steamed rice.

Crispy Lamb with Lettuce

⁂ SERVES 4

⁂ PREPARATION TIME: 15 MINUTES

⁂ COOKING TIME: 20 MINUTES

14 oz lamb backstraps or loin fillets
2 tablespoons light soy sauce
1 tablespoon Chinese rice wine
2 teaspoons fish sauce
1/2 teaspoon sesame oil
2 garlic cloves, crushed
1 teaspoon finely grated fresh ginger
1/3 cup cornstarch
vegetable oil, for deep-frying
12 baby romaine lettuce leaves
plum sauce, to serve
4 scallions, thinly sliced, to serve

Wrap the lamb in plastic wrap and put it in the freezer for 30 minutes, or until semi-frozen. Remove the plastic wrap and cut the lamb lengthways into three thin slices, then thinly slice across the grain, so that you have julienne strips. Place in a bowl with the soy sauce, rice wine, fish sauce, sesame oil, garlic, and ginger. Mix well to coat, then cover and refrigerate for 2 hours.

Sift the cornstarch over the lamb and mix well. Spread the lamb out on a sheet and return to the refrigerator, uncovered, for 1 hour.

Preheat the oven to 300°F. Heat the oil in a wok or deep heavy-based saucepan to 350°F, or until a cube of bread dropped into the oil browns in 15 seconds. Deep-fry the lamb in batches for 5–6 minutes, or until crisp and browned. Lift the lamb out with a slotted spoon and drain on crumpled paper towels. Keep warm in the oven while you cook the remainder.

To serve, cup a lettuce leaf in your hand. With the other hand, drizzle the inside with a little plum sauce, fill with the lamb mixture, and sprinkle with the scallion. Alternatively, arrange the lettuce, lamb, scallion and plum sauce in separate dishes for your guests to assemble their own 'cups'.

Meat Dumplings in Yogurt Sauce

🌿 SERVES 4–6

🌿 PREPARATION TIME: 40 MINUTES

🌿 COOKING TIME: 35 MINUTES

2 cups all-purpose flour
1/4 cup clarified butter, melted, for baking,
    plus 2 tablespoons extra, to serve
    (see Note)
2 garlic cloves, crushed, to serve
1 tablespoon dried mint, to serve

FILLING
1 tablespoon clarified butter
1 small onion, finely chopped
2 tablespoons pine nuts
9 oz ground lamb
pinch ground allspice

YOGURT SAUCE
3 cups plain yogurt
2 teaspoons cornstarch
1 egg white, lightly beaten

To make the dough, sift the flour and 1 teaspoon salt into a bowl and add 3/4 cup water a little at a time, and combine until the mixture comes together in a ball. Cover and allow to rest for 30 minutes.

To make the filling, melt the clarified butter in a deep heavy-based frying pan and cook the onion over medium heat for 5 minutes, or until soft. Add the pine nuts and allow them to brown, stirring constantly. Increase the heat to high and add the lamb and allspice, stirring until the meat changes color. Season and cool.

Preheat the oven to 350°F. Lightly grease two baking sheets. Roll out the dough on a floured board, to about 1/4 inch thick and cut into rounds using a 2 inch cutter. Put a teaspoon of filling in the center of each round and fold the pastry over into a crescent. Press the edges together firmly and then wrap the crescent around one finger and press the two ends together to make a hat shape. Place on the baking sheets and brush lightly with the clarified butter. Bake for 10 minutes, or until lightly browned.

To make the sauce, put the yogurt in a large, heavy-based saucepan and stir until smooth. Combine the cornstarch with 1 1/2 cups water, stir until smooth, then add to the yogurt with the egg white and 2 teaspoons salt. Cook over medium heat, stirring until the mixture thickens. Add the dumplings to the pan, stir gently, then cook, uncovered, over low heat for 10 minutes, stirring occasionally.

Just before serving, melt the extra clarified butter in a small frying pan and pan-fry the garlic gently for a few seconds. Stir in the mint and remove from the heat. Pour over the dumplings and serve with rice.

NOTE: To clarify butter, heat butter over low heat until liquid. Leave until the white milk solids settle to the bottom. Use a spoon to skim off any foam, then strain off the golden liquid, leaving the white solids behind. Discard the solids.

Duck Breast with Wild Rice

※ SERVES 4
※ PREPARATION TIME: 15 MINUTES
※ COOKING TIME: 1 HOUR

1/2 cup wild rice
2 teaspoons oil
1/2 cup roughly chopped pecans
1/2 teaspoon ground cinnamon
1/3 cup long-grain white rice
2 tablespoons finely chopped Italian
    parsley
4 medium scallions, thinly sliced
2 medium duck breasts
zest of 1 orange

DRESSING
1/3 cup olive oil
1 teaspoon grated orange zest
2 tablespoons orange juice
2 teaspoons walnut oil
1 tablespoon chopped preserved ginger

To make the dressing, thoroughly mix the ingredients together and season. Set aside.

Put the wild rice in a saucepan with 1 1/4 cups water. Bring to a boil and cook, covered, for 30 minutes, or until tender. Drain away any excess water.

Meanwhile, heat the oil in a large frying pan. Add the pecans and cook, stirring, until golden. Add the cinnamon and a pinch of salt, and cook for 1 minute.

Bring a large saucepan of water to a boil. Add the white rice and cook, stirring occasionally, for 12 minutes, or until tender. Drain and mix with the wild rice and pecans in a large, shallow bowl. Add the parsley and scallions. Add half the dressing and toss well.

Put the duck, skin side down, in a cold frying pan, then heat the pan over high heat. Cook for 5 minutes, or until crisp, then turn over and cook for another 5 minutes. Tip out any excess fat and add the remaining dressing and the orange zest, and cook until bubbling. Transfer the duck to a serving dish and slice, diagonally. Serve with the rice, drizzled with any juices.

Chicken, Veal and Mushroom Loaf

SERVES 6

PREPARATION TIME: 20 MINUTES

COOKING TIME: 1 HOUR

3½ oz pappardelle
¼ cup fresh breadcrumbs
1 tablespoon dry white wine
13 oz ground chicken
13 oz ground veal
2 garlic cloves, crushed
1 cup finely chopped white mushrooms
2 eggs, beaten
pinch freshly grated nutmeg
pinch cayenne pepper
¼ cup sour cream
4 scallions, finely chopped
2 tablespoons chopped Italian parsley

Grease a 6-cup capacity loaf pan. Cook the pappardelle in a large saucepan of rapidly boiling salted water until *al dente*. Drain.

Preheat the oven to 400°F. Soak the breadcrumbs in the wine. Mix the crumbs in a bowl with the chicken, veal, garlic, mushrooms, eggs, nutmeg, cayenne pepper, then season to taste. Mix in the sour cream, scallion, and parsley.

Place half the ground meat mixture into the prepared pan with your hands. Form a deep trough along the entire length. Fill the trough with the pappardelle. Press the remaining meat mixture over the top. Bake for 50–60 minutes, draining the excess fat and juice from the pan twice during cooking. Cool slightly, then slice.

NOTE: Mushrooms can be chopped in a food processor. Don't prepare too far in advance or they will discolor and darken the loaf.

Circassian Chicken

🔥 SERVES 6

🔥 PREPARATION TIME: 25 MINUTES

🔥 COOKING TIME: 1 HOUR

2 teaspoons paprika

1/4 teaspoon cayenne pepper

1 tablespoon walnut oil

4 chicken breasts, on the bone

4 chicken wings

1 large onion, chopped

2 celery stalks, roughly chopped

1 carrot, chopped

1 bay leaf

4 sprigs Italian parsley

1 sprig thyme

6 peppercorns

1 teaspoon coriander seeds

2 1/2 cups walnuts, toasted (see Note)

2 slices white bread, crusts removed

4 garlic cloves, crushed

1 tablespoon paprika, extra

salad leaves, to serve

Put the paprika and cayenne pepper in a small dry frying pan and heat over low heat for about 2 minutes, or until aromatic. Add the walnut oil to the pan and set aside until ready to use.

Put the chicken pieces in a large saucepan with the onion, celery, carrot, bay leaf, parsley, thyme, peppercorns, and coriander seeds. Add about 4 cups water and bring to a boil. Reduce the heat to low and simmer for 15–20 minutes, or until the chicken is tender. Remove from the heat and allow to cool in the stock. Remove the chicken pieces and return the stock to the heat. Simmer for 20–25 minutes, or until reduced by half. Strain, skim off the fat, and reserve the stock. Remove the chicken skin and shred the flesh into bite-sized pieces. Season well and ladle some stock over the chicken to keep it moist. Set aside.

Reserve a few of the walnuts to use as garnish and blend the rest in a food processor to form a rough paste. Combine the bread with 1/2 cup of the reserved stock, add to the food processor, and mix in short bursts for several seconds. Add the garlic and extra paprika, and season. Process until smooth. Gradually add 1 cup of warm chicken stock until the mixture is of a smooth pourable consistency, adding a little more stock if necessary.

Mix half the sauce with the chicken and place on a serving platter. Pour the rest over to cover, then sprinkle with the spiced walnut mixture and the remaining walnuts. Serve at room temperature on a bed of salad leaves.

NOTE: Californian walnuts are best for this recipe as they are much less bitter than other types of walnut.

San Choy Bau with Noodles

🔥 SERVES 6
🔥 PREPARATION TIME: 20 MINUTES
🔥 COOKING TIME: 15 MINUTES

1 lb 2 oz raw shrimp
vegetable oil, for deep-frying
1 cup dried rice vermicelli (see Notes)
$1/4$ cup chicken stock
2 tablespoons Chinese rice wine
2 tablespoons soy sauce
2 tablespoons hoisin sauce
1 tablespoon brown bean sauce
$1/2$ teaspoon sugar
$1/4$ cup peanut oil
1 medium garlic clove, crushed
1 tablespoon finely chopped fresh ginger
3 medium scallions, thinly sliced
   and green ends reserved, to garnish
$2/3$ cup ground pork (see Notes)
12 iceberg lettuce leaves, trimmed into
   neat cups

Peel the shrimp and gently pull out the dark vein from the back of each shrimp, starting at the head end. Roughly chop.

Fill a deep heavy-based saucepan or deep-fryer one-third full of oil and heat to 325°F, or until a cube of bread dropped into the oil browns in 20 seconds. Add the dried rice vermicelli to the oil in batches and deep-fry until puffed up but not browned — this will only take a few seconds, so watch it carefully. Remove with a slotted spoon and drain well on crumpled paper towels.

To make the stir-fry sauce, put the chicken stock, Chinese rice wine, soy sauce, hoisin sauce, brown bean sauce, sugar and $1/2$ teaspoon salt in a small bowl and stir together until well combined.

Heat the peanut oil in a wok over high heat and swirl to coat. Add the garlic, ginger and scallions and stir-fry for 1 minute, being careful not to burn the garlic.

Add the pork to the wok, breaking up the lumps with the back of a wooden spoon, then cook for 4 minutes. Add the shrimp meat and stir-fry for 2 minutes, or until it begins to change color.

Add the stir-fry sauce and stir until combined. Cook over high heat for 2 minutes, or until the mixture thickens slightly.

Divide the noodles among the lettuce cups, spoon the pork and shrimp mixture over the noodles and garnish with the reserved scallions. Serve at once.

NOTES: Make sure the ground pork is not too lean or the mixture will be dry. When deep-frying the vermicelli, take care not to allow the oil to become too hot or the noodles will expand and brown very quickly. Have everything you need ready before you start deep-frying — a slotted spoon for removing the noodles and a sheet lined with crumpled paper towels. Remember to deep-fry the noodles in small batches as they will dramatically increase in volume when cooked.

Larb

※ SERVES 4–6
※ PREPARATION TIME: 20 MINUTES
※ COOKING TIME: 10 MINUTES

1 tablespoon vegetable oil
2 lemon grass stems, white part only,
    thinly sliced
2 green chilies, finely chopped
1 lb 2 oz lean ground pork or beef
¼ cup lime juice
2 teaspoons finely grated lime zest
2–6 teaspoons chili sauce
lettuce leaves, to serve
3 tablespoons chopped cilantro leaves
2 tablespoons chopped mint
1 small red onion, thinly sliced
⅓ cup unsalted roasted peanuts, chopped
¼ cup crisp-fried garlic

Heat the oil in a wok and stir-fry the lemon grass, chili, and pork or beef over high heat for 6 minutes, or until the meat is cooked, breaking up any lumps. Transfer to a bowl and allow to cool. Add the lime juice, zest, and chili sauce and mix well.

Arrange the lettuce leaves on a serving plate. Stir most of the cilantro, mint, onion, peanuts, and garlic through the meat mixture, spoon over the lettuce and sprinkle the rest of the cilantro, mint, onion, peanuts, and garlic over the top.

NOTE: Larb is a popular dish in Laos and also features in Thai cuisine. It is often made with beef, pork, chicken, duck and even tofu, and is flavored with lime, mint and chili.

Savory Egg Custard

✿ SERVES 6
✿ PREPARATION TIME: 20 MINUTES
✿ COOKING TIME: 30 MINUTES

3/4 cup chopped chicken breast fillets
2 teaspoons sake
2 teaspoons Japanese soy sauce
2 medium leeks, sliced
1 small carrot, sliced
5 cups chopped spinach

CUSTARD
4 cups boiling water
1/2 cup dashi granules
2 tablespoons Japanese soy sauce
6 eggs

Place the chicken pieces into six heatproof bowls. Combine the sake and soy sauce, and pour the mixture over the chicken.

Divide the vegetables between the six bowls.

To make the custard, combine the water and dashi granules in a heatproof bowl and stir to dissolve; cool completely. Combine the dashi, soy sauce and eggs, and strain equal amounts into the six bowls.

Cover the bowls with foil, place them in a steamer, and cook on high for 20–30 minutes. Test the custard by inserting a fine skewer into the center; it is cooked when the skewer comes out with no moisture clinging to it. Serve immediately.

Snails with Garlic and Herb Butter

1³/₄ cups canned snails

¹/₂ cup softened butter

4 medium garlic cloves, crushed

2 tablespoons chopped Italian parsley

2 teaspoons snipped chives

36 snail shells (available from specialty food stores), or use ovenproof ramekins

¹/₄ cup fresh white breadcrumbs

Preheat the oven to 400°F. Rinse the snails under cold water. Drain well and set aside. In a small bowl, combine the butter, garlic, parsley and chives until smooth. Season. Put a small amount of the butter and a snail in each shell. Seal the shells with the remaining butter and sprinkle with the breadcrumbs.

Place the snails on a baking sheet with the open end of the snail facing up so that the butter will not run out of the shell. Bake for 5–6 minutes, or until the butter is bubbling and the breadcrumbs are lightly browned. Serve with crusty baguettes.

Cabbage Rolls

🌺 MAKES 12 LARGE ROLLS

🌺 PREPARATION TIME: 30 MINUTES

🌺 COOKING TIME: 1 HOUR 35 MINUTES

1 tablespoon olive oil, plus 1 cup, extra
1 onion, finely chopped
large pinch ground allspice
1 teaspoon ground cumin
large pinch freshly grated nutmeg
2 bay leaves
1 large head cabbage
1 lb 2 oz ground lamb
1 cup short-grain white rice
4 garlic cloves, crushed
1/3 cup pine nuts, toasted
2 tablespoons chopped mint
2 tablespoons chopped Italian parsley
1 tablespoon currants, chopped
1/3 cup lemon juice
extra virgin olive oil, to drizzle
lemon wedges, to serve

Heat 1 tablespoon of the olive oil in a saucepan, add the onion, and cook over medium heat for 10 minutes, or until golden. Add the allspice, cumin, and nutmeg and cook for 2 minutes, or until fragrant. Remove from the pan.

Bring a very large saucepan of water to a boil and add the bay leaves. Cut the tough outer leaves and about 2 inches of the core from the cabbage, then carefully add the cabbage to the boiling water. Cook it for 5 minutes, then carefully loosen a whole leaf with tongs and remove. Continue to cook and remove the leaves until you reach the core. Drain, reserving the cooking liquid, and set aside to cool.

Take 12 leaves of equal size and cut a small 'V' from the core end of each to remove the thickest part. Trim the firm central veins so the leaf is as flat as possible. Use three-quarters of the remaining leaves to line the base of a very large saucepan.

Combine the lamb, onion mixture, rice, garlic, pine nuts, mint, parsley, and currants in a bowl and season well. With the core end of the leaf closest to you, form 2 tablespoons of the mixture into an oval and place in the center of the leaf. Roll up, tucking in the sides. Repeat with the remaining 11 leaves and filling. Place tightly, in a single layer, in the lined saucepan, seam side down.

Combine 2 1/2 cups of the reserved cooking liquid with the extra olive oil, lemon juice, and 1 teaspoon salt and pour over the rolls (the liquid should just come to the top of the rolls). Lay the remaining cabbage leaves over the top. Cover and bring to a boil over high heat, then reduce the heat, and simmer for 1 1/4 hours, or until the mince and rice are cooked. Carefully remove from the pan with a slotted spoon, then drizzle with the extra virgin olive oil. Serve with the lemon wedges.

Layered Lamb and Bulgur

SERVES 4–6

PREPARATION TIME: 30 MINUTES

COOKING TIME: 55 MINUTES

2 cups bulgur

14 oz ground lamb

1 large onion, finely chopped

1 tablespoon ground cumin

1 teaspoon ground allspice

plain yogurt, to serve

FILLING

1 tablespoon olive oil, plus extra for
   brushing

1 onion, finely chopped

1 teaspoon ground cinnamon

1 tablespoon ground cumin

1 lb 2 oz ground lamb

2/3 cup raisins

2/3 cup pine nuts, toasted

olive oil, for brushing

Soak the bulgurl in cold water for 30 minutes, then drain and squeeze out excess water. Put the lamb, onion, cumin, allspice, and some salt and pepper in a food processor, and process until combined. Add the bulgur and process to a paste. Refrigerate until needed. Preheat the oven to 350°F. Lightly grease a 8 x 12 inch baking dish.

To make the filling, heat the oil in a large frying pan over medium heat and cook the onion for 5 minutes, or until softened. Add the cinnamon and cumin and stir for 1 minute, or until fragrant. Add the lamb, stirring to break up any lumps, and cook for 5 minutes, or until the meat is brown. Stir in the raisins and pine nuts and season, to taste.

Press half the bulgur mixture into the base of the baking dish, smoothing the surface with wet hands. Spread the filling over the top, then cover with the remaining bulgur, again smoothing the top.

Score a diamond pattern in the top of the mixture with a knife and brush with olive oil. Bake for 40 minutes, or until the top is brown. Cool for 10 minutes before cutting into diamond shapes. Serve with yogurt.

Vietnamese Crepes with Pork, Shrimp and Noodles

SERVES 6
PREPARATION TIME: 45 MINUTES
COOKING TIME: 35 MINUTES

1²/₃ cups rice flour
1 teaspoon baking powder
1¹/₂ teaspoons sugar
¹/₂ teaspoon ground turmeric
1 cup coconut milk
3 teaspoons peanut oil
lime wedges, to serve

DIPPING SAUCE
2 tablespoons lime juice
1 tablespoon fish sauce
1 tablespoon superfine sugar
1 small red chili, finely chopped

SALAD
1 carrot, roughly grated
4¹/₄ oz iceberg lettuce, shredded
1 small cucumber, cut into thin batons
1 cup bean sprouts, trimmed
2 large handfuls mint
2 large handfuls cilantro leaves

FILLING
9 oz raw shrimp
1 small red pepper
2³/₄ oz white mushrooms
4 scallions
2³/₄ oz dried rice vermicelli
1 tablespoon peanut oil
1 large onion, thinly sliced
6 garlic cloves, crushed
7 oz ground pork
1 tablespoon light soy sauce
¹/₄ teaspoon ground white pepper

To make the crepe batter, blend the rice flour, baking powder, sugar, turmeric, coconut milk, ¹/₂ teaspoon salt an 1 cup water in a blender to a smooth batter. Cover and leave in a warm place for 2–4 hours.

Mix together all the dipping sauce ingredients in a small bowl.

Toss all the salad ingredients together in a large bowl.

To make the filling, peel the shrimp, gently pull out the dark vein from each shrimp back, starting at the head end, then chop the shrimp meat. Remove the seeds and membrane from the pepper. Thinly slice the pepper, mushrooms, and scallions. Break the vermicelli into pieces and soak in boiling water for 6–7 minutes, or until soft. Drain. Heat a wok over high heat, add the peanut oil, and swirl to coat. Add the onion and cook for 2 minutes, then add the garlic, cooking for a further 30 seconds. Add the pork and cook for 2 minutes, or until browned. Stir in the shrimp, pepper and mushrooms, and cook until the shrimp change color. Stir in the noodles, soy sauce, white pepper, and scallion. Remove from heat.

To make the crepes, whisk the batter until smooth. Heat ¹/₂ teaspoon of the oil in a 12 inch non-stick frying pan. Pour ¹/₃ cup of the batter into the center of the pan, and swirl to spread to the edges. Cook over medium heat for | 1–2 minutes, or until golden and crispy. Turn and repeat on the other side. Repeat with the remaining oil and batter to make six crepes in total.

To assemble, place a portion of the filling on half a crepe, folding the other half on top. Repeat with the remaining crepes and filling. Serve with the dipping sauce, salad, and lime wedges.

Peking Duck with Mandarin Pancakes

🔆 SERVES 6

🔆 PREPARATION TIME: 1 HOUR

🔆 COOKING TIME: 1 HOUR 15 MINUTES

3 lb 12 oz duck, washed

12 cups boiling water

1 tablespoon honey

12 scallions

1 small cucumber, seeded and cut into
    batons

2 tablespoons hoisin sauce

MANDARIN PANCAKES

$2^1/_2$ cups all-purpose flour

2 teaspoons superfine sugar

1 cup boiling water

1 tablespoon sesame oil

Remove the neck and any large pieces of fat from inside the duck carcass. Hold the duck over the sink and very carefully and slowly pour the boiling water over it, rotating the duck. Put the duck on a rack in an ovenproof dish. Mix the honey with $^1/_2$ cup hot water and brush two coats of this glaze all over the duck. Dry in a cool, airy place for about 4 hours.

Preheat the oven to 425°F. Cut a $3^1/_4$ inch section from the white end of each scallion. Make fine parallel cuts from the top of the section towards the white end. Put the scallion pieces in iced water. Roast the duck for 30 minutes, then turn it over without tearing the skin and roast it for 30 minutes. Remove the duck from the oven and leave for a minute or two, then place it on a warm plate.

Meanwhile, to make the pancakes, put the flour and sugar in a bowl and pour in the boiling water. Stir the mixture a few times and leave until lukewarm. Knead the mixture, on a floured surface, into a smooth dough. Cover and set aside for 30 minutes. Take two level tablespoons of dough and roll each one into a ball. Roll out to circles $3^1/_4$ inches in diameter. Brush one of the circles with sesame oil and place the other circle on top. Re-roll to make a thin pancake about 6 inches in diameter. Repeat with the remaining dough and oil to make about 10 'double' pancakes.

Heat a frying pan and cook the pancakes one at a time. When small bubbles appear on the surface, turn the pancake over and cook the second side, pressing the surface with a dish towel. The pancake should puff up when done. Transfer the pancake to a plate. When cool enough to handle, peel the two halves of the double pancake apart. Stack them on a plate and cover.

To serve, thinly slice the duck. Place the pancakes and duck on separate plates. Arrange the cucumber sticks and scallion brushes on another plate. Put the hoisin sauce in a small dish. Spread a little sauce on a pancake, adds some cucumber, a scallion brush, and a piece of duck. Fold over into a neat envelope.

pasta, gnocchi and rice

Spaghetti Carbonara

※ SERVES 6
※ PREPARATION TIME: 10 MINUTES
※ COOKING TIME: 20 MINUTES

1 lb 2 oz spaghetti
8 medium bacon slices
4 eggs
1/2 cup freshly grated parmesan cheese
1 1/4 cups whipping cream
snipped chives, to garnish

Cook the spaghetti in a large saucepan of rapidly boiling salted water until *al dente*. Drain and return to the pan.

While the pasta is cooking, discard the bacon rind and cut the bacon into thin strips. Cook in a heavy-based frying pan over medium heat until crisp. Remove and drain on paper towels.

Beat the eggs, parmesan and cream in a bowl until well combined. Add the bacon and pour the sauce over the warm pasta. Toss gently until pasta is well coated.

Return the pan to the heat and cook over low heat for 1 minute, or until slightly thickened. Season with freshly ground black pepper and serve garnished with snipped chives.

Fettucine Alfredo

※ SERVES 6
※ PREPARATION TIME: 10 MINUTES
※ COOKING TIME: 15 MINUTES

1 lb 2 oz fettucine or tagliatelle
1/3 cup butter
1 1/2 cups freshly grated
   parmesan cheese
1 1/4 cups whipping cream
3 tablespoons chopped Italian parsley

Cook the pasta in a large saucepan of rapidly boiling salted water until *al dente*. Drain and return to the pan.

Meanwhile, heat the butter in a saucepan over low heat. Add the parmesan and cream and bring to a boil, stirring constantly. Reduce the heat and simmer for 10 minutes, or until the sauce has thickened slightly. Add the parsley, season to taste and stir well to combine. Add the sauce to the warm pasta and toss well to combine.

Spaghetti Carbonara

Lemony Herb and Fish Risotto

🌺 SERVES 4–6
🌺 PREPARATION TIME: 20 MINUTES
🌺 COOKING TIME: 30 MINUTES

$1/4$ cup butter
14 oz skinless white fish fillets, cut into
    $1 1/4$ inch cubes
5 cups fish stock
1 medium onion, finely chopped
1 medium garlic clove, crushed
1 teaspoon ground turmeric
$1 1/2$ cups risotto rice
2 tablespoons lemon juice
1 tablespoon chopped Italian parsley
1 tablespoon chopped chives
1 tablespoon chopped dill

Melt half the butter in a frying pan. Add the fish in batches and fry over medium–high heat for 3 minutes, or until the fish is just cooked through. Remove from the pan and set aside.

Pour the fish stock into another pan, bring to a boil, cover and keep at simmering point.

To the first pan, add the remaining butter, onion and garlic and cook over medium heat for 3 minutes, or until the onion is tender. Add the turmeric and stir for 1 minute. Add the rice and stir to coat, then add $1/2$ cup of the fish stock and cook, stirring constantly, over low heat until all the stock has been absorbed. Continue adding $1/2$ cup of stock at a time until all the stock has been added and the rice is translucent, tender and creamy.

Stir in the lemon juice, parsley, chives and dill. Add the fish and stir gently. Serve, maybe garnished with slices of lemon or lime and fresh herb sprigs.

NOTE: The rice must absorb the stock between each addition — the whole process will take about 20 minutes. If you don't have time to make your own stock, you can buy fresh or frozen fish stock from delicatessens, some seafood outlets and most supermarkets.

Spaghetti with Sardines, Fennel and Tomato

🌿 SERVES 4–6

🌿 PREPARATION TIME: 30 MINUTES

🌿 COOKING TIME: 45 MINUTES

3 plum tomatoes

⅓ cup olive oil

3 garlic cloves, crushed

1 cup fresh white breadcrumbs

1 red onion, thinly sliced

1 fennel bulb, quartered, and thinly sliced

⅓ cup raisins

¼ cup pine nuts, toasted

4 anchovy fillets, chopped

½ cup dry white wine

1 tablespoon concentrated tomato purée

4 tablespoons finely chopped Italian parsley

12 oz butterflied sardine fillets

1 lb 2 oz spaghetti

Score a cross in the base of each tomato. Place the tomatoes in a bowl of boiling water for 10 seconds, then plunge into cold water. Drain and peel the skin away from the cross. Cut the tomatoes in half and scoop out the seeds. Roughly chop the tomato flesh.

Heat 1 tablespoon of the oil in a large frying pan over medium heat. Add 1 garlic clove and the breadcrumbs and stir for about 5 minutes, until golden and crisp. Transfer to a plate.

Heat the remaining oil in the same pan and cook the onion, fennel, and the remaining garlic for 8 minutes, or until soft. Add the tomato, raisins, pine nuts, and anchovies and cook for a further 3 minutes. Add the wine, tomato purée and ½ cup water. Simmer for 10 minutes, or until the mixture thickens slightly. Stir in the parsley and set aside.

Pat the sardines dry with paper towels. Cook the sardines in batches in a lightly greased frying pan over medium heat for 1 minute, or until cooked through. Take care not to overcook or they will break up. Set aside.

Cook the pasta in a large saucepan of rapidly boiling salted water until *al dente*. Drain and return to the pan.

Stir the sauce through the pasta until the pasta is well coated and the sauce evenly distributed. Add the sardines and half the breadcrumbs and toss gently. Sprinkle the remaining breadcrumbs over the top and serve immediately.

Parsnip Gnocchi

☀ SERVES 4
☀ PREPARATION TIME: 45 MINUTES
☀ COOKING TIME: 45 MINUTES

1 lb 2 oz parsnip
1 1/2 cups all-purpose flour
1/2 cup freshly grated parmesan cheese

GARLIC HERB BUTTER
1/3 cup butter
2 garlic cloves, crushed
3 tablespoons chopped lemon thyme
1 tablespoon finely grated lime zest

Cut the parsnip into large pieces. Cook in a large saucepan of boiling water for 30 minutes, or until very tender. Drain thoroughly and leave to cool slightly.

Mash the parsnip in a bowl until smooth. Sift the flour into the bowl and add half the parmesan. Season and mix to form a soft dough.

Divide the dough in half. Using floured hands, roll each half of the dough out on a lightly floured surface into a sausage shape 3/4 inch wide. Cut each sausage into short pieces, shape each piece into an oval, and press the top gently with floured fork prongs.

Lower batches of the gnocchi into a large saucepan of boiling salted water. Cook for about 2 minutes, or until the gnocchi rise to the surface. Use a slotted spoon to transfer to serving plates.

To make the garlic herb butter, combine all the ingredients in a small saucepan and cook over medium heat for 3 minutes, or until the butter is nutty brown.

To serve, drizzle the garlic herb butter over the gnocchi and sprinkle with the remaining parmesan cheese.

Red Wine Risotto

※ SERVES 4 AS A STARTER
※ PREPARATION TIME: 20 MINUTES
※ COOKING TIME: 25 MINUTES

2 cups chicken stock
$1/3$ cup butter
1 onion, finely chopped
1 large garlic clove, crushed
2 tablespoons chopped thyme
1 cup risotto rice
2 cups dry red wine
$1/2$ cup freshly grated parmesan cheese

Pour the stock into a saucepan and bring to a boil. Reduce the heat, cover with a lid, and keep at a low simmer.

Melt the butter in a large wide saucepan. Add the onion and garlic and cook until softened but not browned. Add the thyme and rice and stir until the rice is well coated. Season.

Add half the red wine and cook, stirring, until it has all been absorbed. Add $1/2$ cup of the hot stock and stir over medium heat until all the liquid is absorbed. Continue adding more stock, $1/2$ cup at a time until you have used half the stock. Add the remaining red wine to the risotto, stirring until it has been absorbed. Keep adding $1/2$ cup of the stock until all the liquid is absorbed, and the rice is tender and creamy.

Remove the pan from the heat and stir in half the parmesan. Serve with the remaining cheese sprinkled over the top.

Gorgonzola and Toasted Walnuts on Linguine

※ SERVES 4
※ PREPARATION TIME: 15 MINUTES
※ COOKING TIME: 20 MINUTES

$3/4$ cup walnut halves
1 lb 2 oz linguine
$1/4$ cup butter
1 cup crumbled gorgonzola cheese
2 tablespoons whipping cream
1 cup fresh peas

Preheat the oven to 350°F. Lay the walnuts on a baking sheet in a single layer and bake for about 5 minutes, until lightly toasted. Set the walnuts aside to cool.

Cook the linguine in a large saucepan of rapidly boiling salted water until *al dente*. Drain and return to the pan.

While the pasta is cooking, melt the butter in a small saucepan over low heat and add the gorgonzola, cream, and peas. Stir gently for 5 minutes, or until the sauce has thickened. Season to taste. Add the sauce and the walnuts to the pasta and toss until well combined. Serve immediately, sprinkled with pepper.

Red Wine Risotto

Orecchiette with Broccoli

※ SERVES 6
※ PREPARATION TIME: 5 MINUTES
※ COOKING TIME: 15 MINUTES

1 lb 10 oz broccoli, cut into florets
1 lb orecchiette
¼ cup extra virgin olive oil
8 anchovy fillets
½ teaspoon dried chilli flakes
⅓ cup grated pecorino or parmesan
  cheese

Blanch the broccoli in a large saucepan of boiling salted water for 5 minutes, or until just tender. Remove with a slotted spoon, drain well, and return the water to a boil. Cook the pasta in the boiling water until *al dente*, then drain well and return to the pan.

Meanwhile, heat the oil in a heavy-based frying pan and cook the anchovies over very low heat for about 1 minute. Add the chilli and broccoli. Increase the heat to medium and cook, stirring, for 5 minutes, or until the broccoli is well-coated and beginning to break apart. Season. Add to the pasta, add the cheese, and toss.

Spaghetti with Creamy Lemon Sauce

※ SERVES 4
※ PREPARATION TIME: 10 MINUTES
※ COOKING TIME: 20 MINUTES

1 lb 2 oz spaghetti
1 cup whipping cream
¾ cup chicken stock
1 tablespoon finely grated lemon zest, plus
  extra, to garnish
2 tablespoons finely chopped Italian
  parsley
2 tablespoons snipped chives

Cook the spaghetti in a large saucepan of rapidly boiling salted water until *al dente*. Drain and return to the pan.

While the spaghetti is cooking, combine the cream, chicken stock, and lemon zest in a saucepan over medium heat. Bring to a boil, stirring occasionally. Reduce the heat and simmer gently for 10 minutes, or until the sauce is reduced and thickened slightly.

Add the sauce and herbs to the spaghetti and toss to combine. Serve immediately, garnished with extra lemon zest.

Orecchiette with Broccoli

Herb-Filled Ravioli with Sage Butter

❀ SERVES 4
❀ PREPARATION TIME: 1 HOUR
❀ COOKING TIME: 10 MINUTES

PASTA
2½ cups all-purpose flour
3 eggs, beaten
¼ cup olive oil

FILLING
1 cup ricotta cheese
2 tablespoons freshly grated parmesan
    cheese, plus extra, shaved, to garnish
2 teaspoons snipped chives
1 tablespoon chopped Italian parsley
2 teaspoons chopped basil
1 teaspoon chopped thyme

SAGE BUTTER
¾ cup butter
12 sage leaves

Sift the flour into a bowl and make a well in the center. Gradually mix in the eggs and oil. Turn out onto a lightly floured surface and knead for 6 minutes, or until smooth. Cover with plastic wrap and leave for 30 minutes.

Mix together the ricotta, parmesan and herbs. Season.

Divide the dough into four even portions. Lightly flour a large work surface and using a floured long rolling pin, roll out one portion from the center to the edge. Continue, always rolling from in front of you outwards. Rotate the dough often. Fold the dough in half and roll it out again. Continue this process seven times to make a smooth circle of pasta about ¼ inch thick. Roll this sheet out quickly and smoothly to a thickness of ⅛ inch. Make four sheets of pasta, two slightly larger than the others. Cover with a dish towel.

Spread one of the smaller sheets out on a work surface and place heaped teaspoons of filling at 2 inch intervals. Brush a little water between the filling along the cutting lines. Place a larger sheet on top and firmly press the sheets together along the cutting lines. Cut the ravioli with a pastry wheel or knife and transfer to a lightly floured baking sheet. Repeat with the remaining dough and filling.

To make the sage butter, melt the butter over low heat in a small heavy-based saucepan, without stirring or shaking. Pour the clear butter into another container and discard any white sediment. Return the clarified butter to a clean pan and heat gently over medium heat. Add the sage leaves and cook until crisp but not brown. Remove, drain on paper towels and reserve the butter.

Cook the ravioli in batches in a large saucepan of salted simmering water for 5–6 minutes, or until tender. Top with warm sage butter and leaves and garnish with shaved parmesan.

NOTE: Don't cook the ravioli in rapidly boiling water or the squares will split and lose the filling.

Scallops on Asian Risotto Cakes with Pesto

※ SERVES 4
※ PREPARATION TIME: 35 MINUTES
※ COOKING TIME: 40 MINUTES

2 cups vegetable stock

2 tablespoons mirin

1 lemon grass stem, white part only,
  bruised

2 kaffir lime leaves

3 cilantro stems

1 tablespoon fish sauce

1 tablespoon butter

1 tablespoon peanut oil

3 red Asian shallots, thinly sliced

4 scallions, chopped

3 garlic cloves, chopped

2 tablespoons finely chopped fresh ginger

1 teaspoon white pepper

⅔ cup risotto rice

PESTO

2 tablespoons toasted unsalted chopped
  peanuts

1 cup chopped cilantro leaves, plus extra,
  to garnish

2 garlic cloves, chopped

1 teaspoon finely chopped fresh ginger

½ teaspoon white papper

¼ cup lime juice

1–2 teaspoons grated jaggery or unpacked
  brown sugar

1 tablespoon fish sauce

1–2 tablespoons peanut oil

vegetable oil, for pan-frying

all-purpose flour, to dust

16 large white scallops, without roe

lime slices, to serve

Combine the stock, mirin, lemon grass, kaffir lime leaves, cilantro stems, fish sauce, and 1 cup water in a saucepan, bring to a boil, then reduce the heat and keep at a simmer.

To make the risotto, heat the butter and peanut oil in a large saucepan over medium heat until bubbling. Add the shallot, scallion, garlic, ginger, and white pepper and cook for 2–3 minutes, or until fragrant and the onion is soft. Add the rice and stir until coated. Add ½ cup of the stock (avoid the lemon grass and cilantro stems). Stir constantly over medium heat until nearly all the liquid is absorbed. Continue adding the stock ½ cup at a time, stirring constantly, for about 25 minutes, or until all the stock is absorbed and the rice is tender and creamy. Remove from the heat, cool, then cover and refrigerate for 3 hours, or until cold.

To make the pesto, combine the peanuts, cilantro leaves, garlic, ginger, and the white pepper in a blender or food processor and process until finely chopped. With the motor running, slowly add the lime juice, jaggery, fish sauce, and peanut oil and process until smooth — you might not need all the oil.

Divide the risotto into four balls, then mould into patties. Cover and refrigerate for 10 minutes. Heat the vegetable oil in a large frying pan over medium heat. Dust the patties with the flour and cook in batches for 2 minutes on each side, or until crisp. Drain on paper towels. Cover and keep warm.

Heat a little vegetable oil in a clean frying pan over high heat. Cook the scallops in batches for 1 minute on each side. Serve a cake with four scallops, some pesto, and lime slices. Garnish with the extra cilantro leaves.

Fettucine with Zucchini and Crisp-Fried Basil

🌺 SERVES 6
🌺 PREPARATION TIME: 15 MINUTES
🌺 COOKING TIME: 15 MINUTES

1 cup olive oil
1/2 cup basil leaves
1 lb 2 oz fettucine or tagliatelle
1 lb 2 oz zucchinis
1/4 cup butter
2 garlic cloves, crushed
3/4 cup freshly grated parmesan cheese

To crisp-fry the basil leaves, heat the oil in a small frying pan, add two leaves at a time and cook for 1 minute, or until crisp. Remove with a slotted spoon and drain on paper towels. Repeat with the remaining basil leaves.

Cook the fettucine in a large saucepan of rapidly boiling salted water until *al dente*. Drain and return to the pan.

While the pasta is cooking, grate the zucchinis. Heat the butter in a deep heavy-based saucepan over low heat until the butter is foaming. Add the garlic and cook for 1 minute. Add the zucchini and cook, stirring occasionally, for 1–2 minutes or until softened. Add to the hot pasta. Add the parmesan and toss well. Serve the pasta garnished with the crisp basil leaves.

NOTE: The basil leaves can be fried up to 2 hours in advance. Store in an airtight container after cooling.

Blue Cheese Tagliatelle

🌺 SERVES 6
🌺 PREPARATION TIME: 15 MINUTES
🌺 COOKING TIME: 20 MINUTES

2 medium zucchinis
2 tablespoons butter
1 medium garlic clove, crushed
3 1/2 fl oz white wine
3/4 cup crumbled blue cheese
1/4 cup whipping cream
1 lb 2 oz white or green tagliatelle
2–3 tablespoons freshly grated parmesan
    cheese
chopped Italian parsley, to garnish

Slice the zucchinis. Melt the butter in a frying pan. Add the zucchini and garlic and cook until the zucchini is tender. Stir in the wine, cheese, cream, and a pinch of black pepper. Simmer for 10 minutes.

Meanwhile, cook the tagliatelle in a large saucepan of rapidly boiling salted water until *al dente*. Drain, rinse under warm water and drain again.

Return the pasta to the pan. Add the sauce and toss through the pasta for a few minutes over low heat. Serve sprinkled with the parmesan and parsley.

Fettucine with Zucchini and Crisp-Fried Basil

Tomato and Cheese Risotto Cakes

🌿 SERVES 6
🌿 PREPARATION TIME: 30 MINUTES
🌿 COOKING TIME: 40 MINUTES

1 small onion
$1/4$ cup sun-dried tomatoes
1 oz mozzarella cheese
$3^1/4$ cups vegetable stock
1 tablespoon olive oil
1 tablespoon butter
$1^1/4$ cups short-grain rice
$1/3$ cup freshly grated parmesan cheese
vegetable oil, for deep-frying
$2^1/2$ oz mixed salad leaves, to serve

Finely chop the onion. Chop the sun-dried tomatoes and cut the mozzarella cheese into $1/2$ inch cubes.

Bring the stock to a boil in a small saucepan. Reduce the heat, cover, and keep gently simmering.

Heat the olive oil and butter in a heavy-based saucepan. Add the onion and stir over medium heat for 3 minutes, or until golden. Add the rice. Reduce the heat to low and stir for 3 minutes, or until the rice is lightly golden. Add a quarter of the stock to the pan. Stir for 5 minutes, or until all the liquid has been absorbed. Repeat the process until all the stock has been added and the rice is almost tender, stirring constantly. Stir in the parmesan. Remove from the heat, transfer to a bowl to cool, and refrigerate for 1 hour.

With wet hands, roll 2 tablespoons of the rice mixture into a ball. Make an indentation in the ball and press in a cube of mozzarella and a couple of pieces of sun-dried tomato. Re-shape the ball to cover the indentation, then flatten slightly to a disc shape. Repeat the process with the remaining mixture. Refrigerate for 15 minutes.

Fill a deep-fryer or large heavy-based saucepan one-third full of vegetable oil and heat to 350°F, or until a cube of bread dropped into the oil browns in 15 seconds. Gently lower the risotto cakes, a few at a time, into the oil. Cook for 1–2 minutes, or until golden brown. Remove with a slotted spoon and drain on paper towels. Serve the risotto cakes with salad leaves.

Orecchiette with Tuna, Lemon and Caper Sauce

🔥 SERVES 4
🔥 PREPARATION TIME: 10 MINUTES
🔥 COOKING TIME: 20 MINUTES

1 lb 2 oz orecchiette
1½ tablespoons butter
1 garlic clove, crushed
1 onion, finely chopped
15 oz canned tuna in brine, drained
2 tablespoons lemon juice
1 cup whipping cream
2 tablespoons chopped Italian parsley
1 tablespoon capers, drained
¼ teaspoon cayenne pepper (optional)
caperberries, to garnish (optional)

Cook the orecchiette in a large saucepan of rapidly boiling salted water until *al dente*. Drain and return to the pan.

Melt the butter in a saucepan and cook the garlic and onion for 1–2 minutes. Add the tuna, lemon juice, cream, half the parsley, and the capers. Season with black pepper and cayenne pepper, if using. Simmer over low heat for 5 minutes.

Add the tuna sauce to the pasta and toss until thoroughly combined. Serve the pasta sprinkled with the remaining parsley. Garnish with caperberries, if desired.

Creamy Shrimp with Fettucine

🔥 SERVES 4
🔥 PREPARATION TIME: 30 MINUTES
🔥 COOKING TIME: 20 MINUTES

1 lb 2 oz fettucine
1 lb 2 oz raw shrimp
1½ tablespoons butter
1 tablespoon olive oil
6 scallions, chopped
1 garlic clove, crushed
1 cup whipping cream
2 tablespoons chopped Italian parsley,
   to serve

Cook the fettucine in a large saucepan of rapidly boiling water until *al dente*. Drain and return to the pan.

Peel the shrimp and gently pull out the dark vein from each shrimp back, starting from the head end. Heat the butter and oil in a frying pan, add the scallion and garlic and stir over low heat for 1 minute. Add the shrimp and cook for 2–3 minutes, or until the flesh changes color. Remove the shrimp from the pan and set aside. Add the cream to the pan and bring to a boil. Reduce the heat and simmer until the sauce begins to thicken. Return the shrimp to the pan, season to taste, and simmer for 1 minute.

Add the shrimp and sauce to the warm fettucine and toss gently. Serve sprinkled with chopped parsley.

Orecchiette with Tuna, Lemon and Caper Sauce

Penne Alla Napolitana

🌿 SERVES 4–6
🌿 PREPARATION TIME: 20 MINUTES
🌿 COOKING TIME: 25 MINUTES

2 tablespoons olive oil
1 medium onion, finely chopped
2–3 medium garlic cloves, finely chopped
1 small carrot, finely diced
1 medium celery stalk, finely diced
3¼ cups canned chopped tomatoes
    or 5 cups ripe peeled, chopped
    tomatoes
1 tablespoon concentrated tomato purée
3 tablespoons shredded basil
5½ cups penne
freshly grated parmesan cheese, to serve,
    optional

Heat the oil in a large frying pan. Add the onion and garlic and cook for 2 minutes, or until golden. Add the carrot and celery and cook for a further 2 minutes.

Add the tomato and concentrated tomato purée. Simmer for 20 minutes, or until the sauce thickens, stirring occasionally. Stir in the shredded basil and season to taste.

While the sauce is cooking, cook the pasta in a large saucepan of rapidly boiling salted water until *al dente*. Drain well and return to the pan.

Add the sauce to the pasta and mix well. Serve with freshly grated parmesan cheese, if desired.

Spaghetti Puttanesca

🌿 SERVES 6
🌿 PREPARATION TIME: 15 MINUTES
🌿 COOKING TIME: 20 MINUTES

⅓ cup olive oil
2 medium onions, finely chopped
3 medium garlic cloves, finely chopped
½ teaspoon chili flakes
6 large ripe tomatoes, diced
4 tablespoons capers, rinsed and
    squeezed dry
8 anchovy fillets in oil, drained and
    chopped
¾ cup medium Kalamata olives
3 tablespoons chopped Italian parsley
13 oz spaghetti

Heat the olive oil in a saucepan, add the onion and cook over medium heat for 5 minutes. Add the garlic and chili flakes to the saucepan and cook for 30 seconds. Add the tomato, capers and anchovies. Simmer over low heat for 10–15 minutes, or until the sauce is thick and pulpy. Stir the olives and parsley through the sauce.

While the sauce is cooking, cook the spaghetti in a large saucepan of rapidly boiling salted water until *al dente*. Drain and return to the pan.

Add the sauce to the pasta and stir it through. Season to taste and serve immediately.

Penne Alla Napolitana

Mushroom Risotto

⁂ SERVES 6–8
⁂ PREPARATION TIME: 10 MINUTES
⁂ COOKING TIME: 1 HOUR

¾ oz dried porcini mushrooms
4 cups chicken or vegetable stock
2 tablespoons olive oil
⅓ cup butter, chopped
1 lb 7 oz small cap or Swiss brown
     mushrooms, stems trimmed, sliced
3 garlic cloves, crushed
⅓ cup dry white vermouth
1 onion, finely chopped
2 cups risotto rice
1½ cups freshly grated parmesan cheese

Soak the porcini mushrooms in 2 cups warm water for 30 minutes. Drain, retaining the liquid. Chop mushrooms, then pour the liquid through a fine sieve lined with a paper towel.

Put the stock and the mushroom liquid together in a saucepan. Bring to a boil, then reduce the heat, cover, and keep at a low simmer.

Heat half the oil and 2 tablespoons of the butter in a frying pan over high heat. Add all the mushrooms and the garlic to the pan. Cook, stirring, for 10 minutes, or until soft. Reduce the heat to low and cook for a further 5 minutes. Increase the heat, add the vermouth and cook for 2–3 minutes, until evaporated. Set aside.

Heat the remaining olive oil and 1 tablespoon butter in a saucepan. Add the onion and cook for 10 minutes, or until soft. Add the rice and stir for 1–2 minutes, or until coated. Add ½ cup stock to the pan and stir constantly over medium heat until all the liquid is absorbed. Continue adding more stock, ½ cup at a time, stirring, for 20–25 minutes, or until tender. Remove from the heat and stir in the mushrooms, parmesan, and the remaining butter. Season to taste.

Gnocchi Romana

3 cups whole milk
1/2 teaspoon freshly grated nutmeg
2/3 cup semolina
1 egg, beaten
1 1/2 cups freshly grated parmesan cheese
1/4 cup melted butter
1/2 cup whipping cream
1/2 cup freshly grated mozzarella cheese

Line a deep jelly roll tin with parchment paper. Combine the milk and half the nutmeg in a saucepan and season to taste. Bring to a boil, reduce the heat and gradually stir in the semolina. Cook, stirring occasionally, for 5–10 minutes, or until the semolina is very stiff.

Remove the pan from the heat, add the egg and 1 cup of the parmesan. Stir to combine and then spread the mixture in the prepared tin. Refrigerate for 1 hour, or until the mixture is firm.

Preheat the oven to 350°F. Lightly grease a shallow casserole dish. Cut the semolina into rounds using a floured 1 1/2 inch cutter and arrange in the dish.

Pour the melted butter over the top, followed by the cream. Combine the remaining grated parmesan with the mozzarella and sprinkle them on the rounds. Sprinkle with the remaining nutmeg. Bake for 20–25 minutes, or until the mixture is golden.

Rice and Peas (Risi e Bisi)

🌼 SERVES 4
🌼 PREPARATION TIME: 15 MINUTES
🌼 COOKING TIME: 25 MINUTES

6 cups chicken or vegetable stock
2 teaspoons olive oil
3 tablespoons butter
1 small onion, finely chopped
1/2 cup cubed pancetta
2 tablespoons chopped Italian parsley
2 1/2 cups young peas
1 cup risotto rice
1/2 cup freshly grated parmesan cheese

Pour the stock into a saucepan and bring to a boil. Reduce the heat, cover with a lid and keep at a low simmer.

Heat the oil and half the butter in a large wide heavy-based saucepan and cook the onion and pancetta over low heat for 5 minutes until softened. Stir in the parsley and peas and add two ladlefuls of the stock. Simmer for 6–8 minutes.

Add the rice and the remaining stock. Simmer until the rice is *al dente* and most of the stock has been absorbed. Stir in the remaining butter and the parmesan, season and serve.

Garlic Bucatini

🌼 SERVES 4
🌼 PREPARATION TIME: 10 MINUTES
🌼 COOKING TIME: 20 MINUTES

5 1/2 cups bucatini or penne
1/3 cup olive oil
8 medium garlic cloves, crushed
2 tablespoons chopped Italian parsley
freshly grated parmesan cheese, to serve

Cook the bucatini in a large saucepan of rapidly boiling water until *al dente*. Drain and return to the pan.

Heat the olive oil over low heat in a frying pan and add the garlic. Cook for 1 minute before removing from the heat. Add the garlic oil and the parsley to the pasta and toss to distribute thoroughly. Serve with parmesan cheese.

Rice and Peas (Risi E Bisi)

Spaghetti Marinara

❋ SERVES 6
❋ PREPARATION TIME: 40 MINUTES
❋ COOKING TIME: 50 MINUTES

12 mussels

TOMATO SAUCE
2 tablespoons olive oil
1 onion, finely diced
1 carrot, sliced
1 red chili, seeded and chopped
2 garlic cloves, crushed
1¾ cups canned crushed tomatoes
½ cup dry white wine
1 teaspoon sugar
pinch cayenne pepper

¼ cup white wine
¼ cup fish stock
1 garlic clove, crushed
13 oz spaghetti
1½ tablespoons butter
4½ oz small squid tubes, sliced
4½ oz boneless white fish fillets, cubed
7 oz raw shrimp, peeled and deveined
1 large handful Italian parsley, chopped
7 oz canned clams, drained

Scrub the mussels with a stiff brush and pull out the hairy beards. Discard any broken mussels, or open ones that don't close when tapped on the bench. Rinse well.

To make the tomato sauce, heat the oil in a saucepan, add the onion and carrot and stir over medium heat for about 10 minutes, or until the vegetables are lightly browned. Add the chili, garlic, tomato, white wine, sugar, and cayenne pepper. Simmer for 30 minutes, stirring occasionally.

Meanwhile, heat the wine with the stock and garlic in a large saucepan and add the unopened mussels. Cover the pan and shake it over high heat for 3–5 minutes. After 3 minutes, start removing any opened mussels and set them aside. After 5 minutes discard any unopened mussels and reserve the wine mixture.

Cook the pasta in a large saucepan of rapidly boiling salted water until *al dente*. Drain and keep warm.

Melt the butter in a frying pan, add the squid rings, fish and shrimp and stir-fry for 2 minutes. Set aside. Add the reserved wine mixture, mussels, squid, fish, prawns, parsley, and clams to the tomato sauce and reheat gently. Gently combine the sauce with the pasta and serve at once.

Spiced Carrot and Feta Gnocchi

※ SERVES 6–8
※ PREPARATION TIME: 20 MINUTES
※ COOKING TIME: 10 MINUTES

2 lb 4 oz carrots
1⅓ cups crumbled feta cheese
2¼ cups all-purpose flour
¼ teaspoon ground nutmeg
¼ teaspoon garam masala
1 egg, lightly beaten

MINTED CREAM SAUCE
1½ tablespoons butter
2 garlic cloves, crushed
2 scallions, sliced
1 cup whipping cream
2 tablespoons shredded mint

Cut the carrots into large pieces and steam or boil until tender. Drain and allow to cool slightly before transferring to a food processor.

Process the carrot and the feta together until smooth. Transfer the mixture to a large bowl. Stir in the sifted flour, spices, and egg, and mix to form a soft dough.

Lightly coat your fingertips with flour and shape teaspoons of the mixture into flat circles.

To make the minted cream sauce, melt the butter in a frying pan, add the garlic and scallion, and cook over medium heat for 3 minutes, or until the garlic is soft and golden. Add the cream, bring to a boil, then reduce the heat and simmer for 3 minutes, or until the cream has thickened slightly. Remove from the heat and stir through the mint.

Meanwhile, cook the gnocchi, in batches, in a large saucepan of boiling salted water for about 2 minutes, or until they float to the surface. Use a slotted spoon to transfer to warmed serving plates. Drizzle the minted cream sauce over the gnocchi and serve.

NOTE: This mixture is not as firm as some other gnocchi recipes. Make sure the dough is put on a lightly floured surface and keep your fingertips coated in flour when you are shaping the gnocchi.

Tagliatelle with Chicken Livers and Cream

13 oz tagliatelle
10½ oz chicken livers
2 tablespoons olive oil
1 medium onion, finely chopped
1 medium garlic clove, crushed
1 cup whipping cream
1 tablespoon snipped chives
1 teaspoon wholegrain mustard
2 eggs, beaten
freshly grated parmesan cheese, to serve
snipped chives, to serve

Cook the tagliatelle in a large saucepan of rapidly boiling salted water until *al dente*. Drain and return to the pan.

While the pasta is cooking, trim any green or discolored parts from the chicken livers, then slice them. Heat the olive oil in a large frying pan. Add the onion and garlic and stir over low heat until the onion is tender.

Add the chicken liver to the pan and cook gently for 2–3 minutes. Remove from the heat and stir in the cream, chives and mustard and season to taste. Return to the heat and bring to a boil. Add the beaten eggs and stir quickly to combine. Remove from the heat.

Add the sauce to the hot pasta and toss well to combine. Serve sprinkled with parmesan and snipped chives.

Linguine Pesto

🔥 SERVES 4–6
🔥 PREPARATION TIME: 15 MINUTES
🔥 COOKING TIME: 15 MINUTES

2 cups firmly packed basil
2 medium garlic cloves, crushed
1/4 cup pine nuts, toasted
3/4 cup olive oil
1/2 cup freshly grated parmesan cheese,
    plus extra, to serve
1 lb 2 oz linguine

Process the basil, garlic and pine nuts together in a food processor. With the motor running, add the oil in a steady stream until mixed to a smooth paste. Transfer to a bowl, stir in the parmesan and season to taste.

Cook the pasta in a large saucepan of rapidly boiling salted water until *al dente*. Drain and return to the pan. Toss enough of the pesto through the pasta to coat it well. Serve sprinkled with parmesan.

NOTE: Refrigerate any leftover pesto in an airtight jar for up to a week. Cover the surface with a layer of oil. Freeze for up to a month.

Spaghetti Clams

🔥 SERVES 4
🔥 PREPARATION TIME: 25 MINUTES
🔥 COOKING TIME: 35 MINUTES

5 cups small clams in shell or
    canned clams in brine
1 tablespoon lemon juice
1/3 cup olive oil
3 medium garlic cloves, crushed
3 1/2 cups canned crushed
    tomatoes
9 oz spaghetti
4 tablespoons chopped Italian parsley

If using fresh clams, clean thoroughly. Place in a large saucepan with the lemon juice. Cover the pan and shake over medium heat for 7–8 minutes until the shells open, discarding any clams that don't open. Remove the clam flesh from the shell of the opened clams and set aside; discard the empty shells. If using canned clams, drain, rinse well and set aside.

Heat the oil in a large saucepan. Add the garlic and cook over low heat for 5 minutes. Add the tomato and stir to combine. Bring to a boil and simmer, covered, for 20 minutes. Add freshly ground black pepper, to taste, and the clams, and stir until heated through.

While the sauce is cooking, cook the spaghetti in a large saucepan of rapidly boiling salted water until *al dente*. Drain and return to the pan. Gently stir in the sauce and the chopped parsley until combined.

Linguine Pesto

Fennel Risotto Balls with Cheesy Filling

※ SERVES 6–8

※ PREPARATION TIME: 30 MINUTES

※ COOKING TIME: 50 MINUTES

6 cups vegetable stock
1 tablespoon oil
2 tablespoons butter
2 medium garlic cloves, crushed
1 medium onion, finely chopped
2 medium fennel bulbs, thinly sliced
1 tablespoon balsamic vinegar
1/2 cup dry white wine
3 cups risotto rice
1/2 cup freshly grated parmesan cheese
1/2 cup snipped chives
1 egg, lightly beaten
1 cup chopped sun-dried tomatoes
2/3 cup cubed mozzarella cheese
1/2 cup frozen peas, thawed
1/2 cup all-purpose flour, seasoned
3 eggs, extra
2 cups dry breadcrumbs
oil, for deep-frying

Pour the stock into a saucepan and bring to a boil. Reduce the heat, cover with a lid and keep at a low simmer.

Heat the oil and butter in a large saucepan and cook the garlic and onion over medium heat for 3 minutes, or until softened but not browned. Add the fennel and cook for 10 minutes, or until it starts to caramelize. Add the vinegar and wine, increase the heat and boil until the liquid evaporates. Stir in the rice until well coated.

Add 1/2 cup hot stock, stirring constantly over medium heat until the liquid is absorbed. Continue adding more stock, 1/2 cup at a time, stirring, for 20–25 minutes, or until all the stock is absorbed and the rice is tender and creamy.

Remove from the heat and stir in the parmesan, chives, egg and tomato. Transfer to a bowl, cover and cool. Put the mozzarella and peas in a bowl and mash together. Season.

Put the flour in one bowl, the extra eggs in another and the breadcrumbs in a third. Lightly beat the eggs. With wet hands, shape the risotto into 14 even balls. Flatten each ball out, slightly indenting the center. Put a heaped teaspoon of the pea mash into the indentation, then shape the rice around the filling to form a ball. Roll each ball in seasoned flour, then dip in the extra egg and roll in breadcrumbs. Place on a foil-covered tray and refrigerate for 30 minutes.

Fill a deep-fryer or large saucepan one-third full of oil and heat to 350°F, or until a cube of bread dropped into the oil browns in 15 seconds. Cook the risotto balls in batches for 5 minutes, or until golden and crisp and the cheese has melted inside. Drain on crumpled paper towels and season with salt. If the cheese has not melted by the end of the cooking time, cook the balls on a tray in a 350°F oven for 5 minutes. Serve with a salad.

Creamy Seafood Ravioli

🌺 SERVES 4
🌺 PREPARATION TIME: 1 HOUR
🌺 COOKING TIME: 30 MINUTES

PASTA DOUGH
2 cups all-purpose flour
3 eggs
1 tablespoon olive oil

FILLING
1/4 cup butter, softened
3 garlic cloves, finely chopped
2 tablespoons finely chopped Italian
    parsley
3 1/2 oz scallops, cleaned and finely
    chopped
3 1/2 oz raw shrimp meat, finely chopped
1 egg yolk

SAUCE
1/4 cup butter
3 tablespoons all-purpose flour
1 1/2 cups milk
10 1/2 fl oz whipping cream
1/2 cup dry white wine
1/2 cup freshly grated parmesan cheese
2 tablespoons chopped Italian parsley

To make the pasta dough, sift the flour and a pinch of salt into a bowl and make a well in the center. Whisk the eggs, oil, and 1 tablespoon water in a bowl, then add gradually to the flour and mix to a firm dough. Gather into a ball.

Knead on a lightly floured surface for 5 minutes, or until smooth and elastic. Transfer to a lightly oiled bowl, cover with plastic wrap, and set aside for 30 minutes.

To make the filling, mix together the butter, garlic, parsley, scallops, and shrimp meat. Set aside.

Roll out a quarter of the pasta dough at a time until very thin (each portion of dough should be roughly 4 inches wide when rolled). Place 1 teaspoonful of filling at 2 inch intervals down one side of each strip. Whisk the egg yolk with 1/4 cup water. Brush along one side of the dough and between the filling. Fold the dough over the filling to meet the other side. Repeat with the remaining filling and dough. Press the edges of the dough together firmly to seal.

Cut between the mounds with a knife or a fluted pastry cutter. Cook, in batches, in a large saucepan of rapidly boiling salted water for 6 minutes each batch. Drain well and return to the pan to keep warm.

To make the sauce, melt the butter in a saucepan, add the flour, and cook over low heat for 2 minutes. Remove from the heat and stir in the combined milk, cream, and wine. Cook over low heat until the sauce begins to thicken, stirring constantly. Bring to a boil and simmer gently for 5 minutes. Add the parmesan and parsley and stir until combined. Remove from the heat, add to the ravioli and toss well.

NOTE: The pasta dough is set aside for 30 minutes to let the gluten in the flour relax. If you don't do this, you run the risk of making tough pasta.

Spaghettini with Garlic and Chili

🔆 SERVES 4–6
🔆 PREPARATION TIME: 10 MINUTES
🔆 COOKING TIME: 20 MINUTES

1 lb 2 oz spaghettini
½ cup extra virgin olive oil
2–3 medium garlic cloves, finely chopped
1–2 medium red chilies, seeded and finely
    chopped
3 tablespoons chopped Italian parsley
freshly grated parmesan cheese, to serve

Cook the spaghettini in a large saucepan of rapidly boiling salted water until *al dente*. Drain and return to the pan.

Meanwhile, heat the extra virgin olive oil in a large frying pan. Add the garlic and chili, and cook over very low heat for 2–3 minutes, or until the garlic is golden. Take care not to burn the garlic or chili as this will make the sauce bitter.

Toss the parsley and the oil, garlic and chili mixture through the pasta. Season. Serve with the parmesan.

Cheese Tortellini with Nutty Herb Sauce

🔆 SERVES 4–6
🔆 PREPARATION TIME: 15 MINUTES
🔆 COOKING TIME: 15 MINUTES

4½ cups ricotta-filled fresh or
    dried tortellini or ravioli
¼ cup butter
¾ cup finely chopped walnuts
⅔ cup pine nuts
2 tablespoons chopped Italian parsley
2 teaspoons thyme
¼ cup ricotta cheese
¼ cup whipping cream

Add the pasta to a large saucepan of rapidly boiling water and cook until *al dente*. Drain and return to the pan.

To make the sauce, heat the butter in a heavy-based frying pan over medium heat until foaming. Add the walnuts and pine nuts and stir for 5 minutes, or until golden brown. Add the parsley, thyme and season.

Beat the ricotta with the cream. Add the sauce to the pasta and toss well to combine. Top with a dollop of ricotta cream. Serve immediately.

Spaghettini with Garlic and Chili

Spinach and Ricotta Gnocchi

🍃 SERVES 4–6

🍃 PREPARATION TIME: 45 MINUTES

🍃 COOKING TIME: 30 MINUTES

4 slices white bread
$1/2$ cup whole milk
10 cups frozen spinach, thawed
1 cup ricotta cheese
2 eggs
$1/2$ cup freshly grated parmesan cheese
$1/4$ cup all-purpose flour
parmesan cheese shavings, to serve

Remove the crust from the bread and soak the bread in the milk, in a shallow dish, for 10 minutes. Squeeze out all the excess liquid. Squeeze the excess liquid from the spinach.

Combine the bread in a bowl with the spinach, ricotta, eggs and parmesan, then season. Use a fork to mix thoroughly. Cover and refrigerate for 1 hour.

Lightly dust your hands in flour. Roll heaped teaspoonfuls of the mixture into dumplings. Lower batches of the gnocchi into a large saucepan of boiling salted water. Cook for about 2 minutes, or until the gnocchi rise to the surface. Transfer to serving plates. Drizzle with foaming butter, if you wish, and serve with the parmesan shavings.

Pasta and Spinach Timbales

🍃 SERVES 6

🍃 PREPARATION TIME: 25 MINUTES

🍃 COOKING TIME: 45 MINUTES

2 tablespoons butter
1 tablespoon olive oil
1 medium onion, chopped
$2^1/2$ cups spinach, steamed and well drained
8 eggs, lightly beaten
1 cup whipping cream
$3^1/2$ oz spaghetti or taglioni, cooked
$1/2$ cup grated cheddar cheese
$1/2$ cup freshly grated parmesan cheese

Preheat the oven to 350°F. Brush six 1-cup ramekins with some melted butter or oil. Line the bases with parchment paper. Heat the butter and oil together in a frying pan. Add the onion and stir over low heat until the onion is tender. Add the well-drained spinach and cook for 1 minute. Remove from the heat and leave to cool. Whisk in the eggs and cream. Stir in the spaghetti and grated cheeses then season to taste. Stir well and spoon into the prepared ramekins.

Place the ramekins in an ovenproof dish. Pour boiling water into the dish to come halfway up the sides of the ramekins. Bake for 30–35 minutes, or until set. Halfway through cooking you may need to cover the top with foil to prevent excess browning. Near the end of cooking time, test the timbales with the point of a knife. When cooked, the knife should come out clean.

Allow the timbales to rest for 15 minutes before turning them out. Run the point of a knife around the edge of each ramekin. Invert onto serving plates.

Spinach and Ricotta Gnocchi

pastry

Winter Squash Tarts

🔥 SERVES 6

🔥 PREPARATION TIME: 30 MINUTES

🔥 COOKING TIME: 20 MINUTES

2 cups all-purpose flour

½ cup chilled butter, cubed

⅓ cup iced water

2 lb 12 oz winter squash, cut into 2½ inch pieces

½ cup sour cream or cream cheese

sweet chili sauce, to serve

Sift the flour and a pinch of salt into a large bowl. Using your fingertips, rub in the butter until the mixture resembles fine breadcrumbs. Make a well in the center, add the iced water, and mix with a flat-bladed knife, using a cutting action, until the mixture comes together in beads. Gently gather the dough together and lift out onto a lightly floured work surface. Press into a ball, then flatten slightly into a disc, wrap in plastic wrap and refrigerate for 30 minutes.

Preheat the oven to400°F. Divide the pastry into six portions, roll each one out, and fit into a 4 inch pie pan. Trim the edge and prick the bases all over with a fork. Bake on a baking sheet for 15 minutes, or until lightly golden, pressing down any pastry that puffs up. Cool, then remove from the pans.

Meanwhile, steam the winter squash for about 15 minutes, or until tender.

Place a tablespoon of sour cream or cream cheese in the middle of each pastry case and stack the squash pieces on top. Season and drizzle with sweet chili sauce to taste. Return to the oven for a couple of minutes to heat through. Serve immediately.

Sweet Potato, Feta and Pine Nut Strudel

❈ SERVES 6

❈ PREPARATION TIME: 25 MINUTES

❈ COOKING TIME: 55 MINUTES

3 cups sweet potato, cut into ¾ inch cubes
1 tablespoon olive oil
½ cup pine nuts, toasted (see Note)
1⅔ cups crumbled feta cheese
2 tablespoons chopped basil
4 medium scallions, chopped
2⅔ tablespoons melted butter
2 tablespoons olive oil, extra, for brushing
7 sheets filo pastry
2–3 teaspoons sesame seeds

Preheat the oven to 350°F. Brush the sweet potato with oil and bake for 20 minutes, or until softened and slightly colored. Transfer to a bowl and cool slightly.

Add the pine nuts, feta, basil and scallions to the bowl, mix gently and season to taste.

Mix the butter and extra oil. Remove one sheet of filo and cover the rest with a damp dish towel to prevent them from drying out. Brush each sheet of filo with the butter mixture and layer them into a pile.

Spread the prepared filling in the center of the filo, covering an area about 4 x 12 inches. Fold the sides of the pastry into the center, then tuck in the ends. Carefully turn the strudel over and place on a baking sheet, seam side down. Lightly brush the top with the butter mixture and sprinkle with sesame seeds. Bake for 35 minutes, or until the pastry is crisp and golden. Serve warm.

NOTE: To toast pine nuts, dry-fry them in a frying pan, stirring and watching them constantly so they don't burn.

Fish Wellington

🌿 SERVES 6
🌿 PREPARATION TIME: 30 MINUTES
🌿 COOKING TIME: 1 HOUR 15 MINUTES

$2^2/_3$ tablespoons butter

3 medium onions, thinly sliced

2 x $10^1/_2$ oz skinless firm white fish
   fillets (each12 inches long)

$^1/_2$ teaspoon sweet paprika

2 medium red bell peppers, quartered,
   seeded and membrane removed

1 large eggplant, cut into $^1/_2$ inch thick
   slices

2 sheets frozen puff pastry, thawed

$^1/_3$ cup dry breadcrumbs

1 egg, lightly beaten

1 cup plain yogurt

1–2 tablespoons chopped dill

Melt the butter in a saucepan, add the sliced onion and stir to coat. Cover and cook over low heat, stirring occasionally, for 15 minutes. Uncover and cook, stirring, for 15 minutes, or until the onion is very soft and lightly browned. Cool, then season to taste.

Rub one side of each fish fillet with paprika. Place one on top of the other, with the paprika on the outside. If the fillets have a thin and a thick end, sandwich together so the thickness is even along the length (thin ends on top of thick ends).

Cook the red pepper quarters, skin side up, under a hot broiler until the skin blackens and blisters. Cool in a plastic bag, then peel. Place the eggplant on a greased baking sheet and brush with oil. Sprinkle with salt and pepper. Broil until golden, then turn to brown the other side.

Preheat the oven to 425°F. Roll the pastry out on a lightly floured surface until large enough to enclose the fish, about 10 x 14 inches. The pastry size and shape will be determined by the fish. Sprinkle the breadcrumbs lengthways along the center of the pastry and place the fish over the breadcrumbs. Top with the onion, then a layer of red pepper, followed by a layer of eggplant.

Brush the pastry edges with beaten egg. Fold the pastry over, pinching firmly together to seal. Use any trimmings to decorate. Brush with egg, then bake for 30 minutes. Cover loosely with foil if the pastry is overbrowning. Slice to serve.

Mix the yogurt and dill with a little salt and pepper in a bowl. Serve with the Wellington.

Cheese and Mushroom Pies

🌿 SERVES 6

🌿 PREPARATION TIME: 40 MINUTES

🌿 COOKING TIME: 30 MINUTES

2⅔ tablespoons butter

2 medium garlic cloves, crushed

5½ cups sliced white mushrooms

1 small red bell pepper, seeded,
    membrane removed and finely chopped

⅔ cup sour cream

3 teaspoons wholegrain mustard

½ cup finely grated gruyère
    or cheddar cheese

6 sheets frozen puff pastry, thawed

½ cup finely grated gruyère
    or cheddar cheese, extra

1 egg, lightly beaten, to glaze

Preheat the oven to 375°F. Lightly grease two baking sheets with melted butter or oil. Heat the butter in a large frying pan. Add the garlic and mushrooms and cook over medium heat, stirring occasionally, until the mushrooms are tender and the liquid has evaporated. Remove from the heat and cool. Stir in the red pepper.

Combine the sour cream, mustard and cheese. Cut 12 circles with a 5½ inch diameter from the pastry. Spread the cream mixture over six of the circles, leaving a ½ inch border. Top each with mushroom mixture. Sprinkle each with 2 teaspoons of the extra cheese. Brush the outer edges with beaten egg then place the reserved pastry rounds on top of the filling, sealing the edges with a fork. Brush the tops of the pastry with egg. Sprinkle the remaining cheese over the pastry. Place the pies on baking sheets and bake for 20 minutes, or until lightly browned and puffed.

Tapenade and Anchovy Tartlets

🌿 SERVES 4

🌿 PREPARATION TIME: 15 MINUTES

🌿 COOKING TIME: 10 MINUTES

1 lb 2 oz block ready-made puff pastry,
    thawed

½ cup ready-made tapenade

1¾ oz canned anchovies, drained

⅓ cup freshly grated parmesan cheese

½ cup freshly grated mozzarella cheese

Divide the pastry into two portions. Roll each portion between two sheets of parchment paper. If making four tartlets, cut out two 4½ inch circles of pastry from each portion, or for two long tartlets roll each portion of pastry into a rectangle 4½ x 10 inches.

Preheat the oven to 400°F. Spread the tapenade evenly over the pastry shapes, leaving a ⅝ inch border. Cut the anchovies into thin strips and arrange them over the top of the tapenade. Sprinkle the parmesan and mozzarella over the top. Bake for 10 minutes, or until risen and golden.

Cheese and Mushroom Pies

Roast Pepper Rice Tarts

❀ SERVES 6
❀ PREPARATION TIME: 45 MINUTES
❀ COOKING TIME: 1 HOUR 5 MINUTES

4 cups vegetable stock
1 tablespoon butter
$1/2$ cup wild rice
$2/3$ cup short-grain brown rice
1 egg, lightly beaten with 1 egg yolk
$1/2$ cup freshly grated parmesan cheese
2 green peppers
2 red peppers
2 yellow peppers
$5^{1/2}$ oz camembert cheese, thinly sliced
2 tablespoons oregano

Grease six 4 inch loose-based fluted tart pans. Pour the stock into a saucepan and bring to a boil. Reduce the heat, cover, and keep at a low simmer.

Melt the butter in a large saucepan over low heat, then stir in the rice until well coated. Add $1/2$ cup of the hot stock to the rice, stirring well. Increase the heat to medium and add the remaining stock, 1 cup at a time, stirring, until it has been absorbed — this will take about 30 minutes. Remove from the heat and cool. Add the egg and parmesan and season to taste.

Divide the rice mixture among the prepared tart pans and press it around the base and sides. Allow to cool completely. Preheat the oven to 400°F.

Cut the peppers in half and remove the seeds and membrane, then cut into large, flattish pieces. Broil or hold over a gas flame until the skin blackens and blisters. Put on a cutting board, cover with a dish towel and allow to cool. Peel off the skin and cut the flesh into smaller pieces. Mix together.

Put the camembert slices in the bottom of the rice-lined pans and divide the pepper evenly among the tarts. Bake for 30 minutes. Sprinkle the oregano over the top and serve hot.

Vol~Au~Vents

🌸 MAKES 4
🌸 PREPARATION TIME: 20 MINUTES
🌸 COOKING TIME: 30 MINUTES

2 sheets frozen puff pastry,
    thawed
1 egg, lightly beaten

SAUCE AND FILLING
2²/₃ tablespoons butter
2 medium scallions, finely chopped
2 tablespoons all-purpose flour
1¹/₂ cups whole milk
your choice of filling (see Note)

Preheat the oven to 425°F. Line a baking sheet with parchment paper. Roll out the pastry to an 8 inch square. Cut four circles of pastry with a 4 inch cutter. Place the rounds onto the sheet and cut 2¹/₂ inch circles into the center of the rounds with a cutter, taking care not to cut right through the pastry. Place the baking sheet in the refrigerator for 15 minutes.

Using a floured knife blade, "knock up" the sides of each pastry round by making even indentations about ¹/₂ inch apart around the circumference. This should allow even rising of the pastry as it cooks. The dough can be made ahead of time up to this stage and frozen until needed.

Carefully brush the pastry with the egg, avoiding the "knocked up" edge as any glaze spilt on the sides will stop the pastry from rising. Bake for 15–20 minutes, or until the pastry has risen and is golden brown and crisp. Cool on a wire rack. Remove the center from each pastry circle and pull out and discard any partially cooked pastry from the center. The pastry can be returned to the oven for 2 minutes to dry out if the center is undercooked. The pastry cases are now ready to be filled with a hot filling before serving.

To make the sauce, melt the butter in a saucepan, add the scallions and stir over low heat for 2 minutes, or until soft. Add the flour and stir for 2 minutes, or until lightly golden. Gradually add the milk, stirring until smooth. Stir constantly over medium heat for 4 minutes, or until the mixture boils and thickens. Season well. Remove and stir in your choice of filling (see Note).

NOTE: Add 2 cups of any of the following to your white sauce: sliced, cooked mushrooms; peeled, deveined and cooked shrimp; chopped, cooked chicken breast; poached, flaked salmon; cooked and dressed crabmeat; oysters; steamed asparagus spears.

Tunisian Brik

❁ SERVES 2
❁ PREPARATION TIME: 30 MINUTES
❁ COOKING TIME: 20 MINUTES

3 tablespoons butter
1 small onion, finely chopped
7 oz canned tuna in oil, drained
1 tablespoon tiny capers, rinsed and
    chopped
2 tablespoons finely chopped Italian
    parsley
2 tablespoons grated parmesan cheese
6 sheets filo pastry
2 small eggs

Preheat the oven to 400°F. Melt 1½ tablespoons butter in a small frying pan and cook the onion over low heat for 5 minutes, or until soft but not brown. Combine the onion, tuna, capers, parsley, and parmesan in a bowl and season.

Cut the filo pastry sheets in half widthways. Melt the remaining butter. Layer four of the half sheets together, brushing each with melted butter. Keep the remaining pastry covered with a damp dish towel. Spoon half the tuna mixture onto one end of the buttered pastry, leaving a border. Make a well in the center of the mixture and break an egg into the well, being careful to leave it whole.

Layer two more sheets of filo together, brushing with melted butter, and place on top of the tuna and egg. Fold in the pastry sides, then roll into a firm parcel, keeping the egg whole. Place on a lightly greased baking sheet and brush with melted butter. Repeat with the remaining pastry, filling, and egg. Bake for 15 minutes, or until the pastry is golden brown. Serve warm or at room temperature.

Smoked Cod Tart

- SERVES 6
- PREPARATION TIME: 30 MINUTES
- COOKING TIME: 55 MINUTES

PASTRY

1 cup all-purpose flour
1/4 cup butter, chopped
1 egg, lightly beaten
1 tablespoon lemon juice
1–2 tablespoons iced water

FILLING

10 1/2 oz smoked cod or haddock fillets
3 eggs, lightly beaten
1/2 cup whipping cream
1/2 cup grated cheddar cheese
1 tablespoon chopped dill

Preheat the oven to 425°F. Lightly grease an 8 1/2 inch diameter loose-based fluted tart pan.

To make the pastry, sift the flour into a large bowl. Using your fingertips, rub in the butter until the mixture resembles fine breadcrumbs. Make a well in the center and add the egg, lemon juice, and most of the iced water. Mix with a flat-bladed knife, using a cutting action, until the mixture comes together in beads. Add more water if the dough is too dry. Gently gather the dough together into a ball, flatten into a disc, and wrap in plastic wrap. Refrigerate for 20 minutes.

Roll out the dough between two sheets of parchment paper until large enough to cover the base and side of the pan. Remove the top sheet of paper and put the pastry in the pan, pressing into the sides. Line with parchment paper large enough to cover the base and sides and spread a layer of baking beads or uncooked rice over the top. Bake for 10 minutes, remove the paper and beads, and bake for another 5 minutes, or until golden. Remove and cool slightly. Reduce the oven to 350°F.

To make the filling, put the cod in a frying pan and cover with water. Bring to a boil, reduce the heat, and simmer for 10–15 minutes, or until the cod flakes easily when tested with a fork. Drain on crumpled paper towels, then allow to cool.

Flake the cod into small pieces, using a fork. Combine the eggs, cream, cheddar, and dill in a bowl, add the cod and mix well. Spoon into the pastry shell and bake for 40 minutes, or until set. Serve the tart hot or cold with lemon or lime wedges and a green salad.

Cherry Tomato and Pesto Tart

❀ SERVES 4
❀ PREPARATION TIME: 15 MINUTES
❀ COOKING TIME: 10 MINUTES

1 lb 2 oz block ready-made puff pastry,
    thawed
1/2 cup ready-made pesto
13 oz cherry tomatoes
2 scallions, finely sliced, plus extra,
    to garnish
extra virgin olive oil, to drizzle

Divide the pastry into two portions. Roll each portion between two sheets of parchment paper. If making four tartlets, cut out two 4$\frac{1}{2}$ inch circles of pastry from each portion, or for two long tartlets roll each portion of pastry into a rectangle 4$\frac{1}{2}$ x 10 inches.

Preheat the oven to 400°F. Spread the pesto over the pastry shapes, leaving a $\frac{5}{8}$ inch border. Top with the cherry tomatoes and finely sliced scallion. Season and bake for 10 minutes, or until golden. Drizzle with extra virgin olive oil and garnish with the scallion slices. Serve warm or hot.

Free-Form Shrimp Pies

❀ SERVES 4
❀ PREPARATION TIME: 20 MINUTES
❀ COOKING TIME: 30 MINUTES

2 cups all-purpose flour
1/2 cup chilled butter, cubed
1/4 cup iced water
1 tablespoon oil
2 inch piece fresh ginger, grated
3 garlic cloves, crushed
2 lb 4 oz raw shrimp, peeled
1/3 cup sweet chili sauce
1/3 cup lime juice
1/3 cup double cream
1/2 cup chopped cilantro leaves
1 egg yolk, lightly beaten, to glaze
lime zest strips, to garnish

Sift the flour into a bowl. Rub in the butter. Add the water and mix. Gather the dough together and lift out onto a lightly floured surface. Press into a ball and flatten into a disc. Wrap in plastic wrap and chill for 15 minutes. Preheat the oven to 400°F. Grease two baking sheets.

Heat the oil in a large frying pan and fry the ginger, garlic, and shrimp for 2–3 minutes. Remove the shrimp and set aside. Add the chili sauce, lime juice, and cream to the pan and simmer until the sauce has reduced by about one-third. Return the shrimp to the pan and add the cilantro. Cool. Divide the pastry into four and roll out each portion, between sheets of parchment paper, into an 8 inch circle. Divide the filling into four and place a portion in the center of each pastry circle, leaving a wide border. Fold the edges over the filling. Brush the pastry with the egg yolk. Bake for 25 minutes, or until golden. Serve with lime zest.

Cherry Tomato and Pesto Tart

Pissaladière

※ SERVES 8

※ PREPARATION TIME: 50 MINUTES

※ COOKING TIME: 2 HOUR

2 teaspoons dried yeast

1 teaspoon sugar

2½ cups white bread flour

2 tablespoons milk powder

1 tablespoon vegetable oil

TOMATO AND ONION TOPPING

⅓ cup olive oil

3–4 medium garlic cloves, finely chopped

6 medium onions, cut into thin rings

1¾ cup canned chopped tomatoes

1 tablespoon concentrated tomato purée

½ cup chopped Italian parsley

1 tablespoon chopped thyme

½ cup canned anchovy fillets,
    drained and halved lengthways

36 small black olives

Lightly grease two 12 inch pizza sheets. Put the yeast, sugar and 1 cup warm water in a small bowl and stir well. Leave in a warm, draught-free place for 10 minutes, or until bubbles appear on the surface. The mixture should be frothy and slightly increased in volume. If your yeast doesn't foam, it is dead, so you will have to discard it and start again.

Sift 2 cups of the flour, the milk powder and ½ teaspoon salt into a large bowl and make a well in the center. Add the oil and yeast mixture and mix thoroughly. Turn out onto a lightly floured surface and knead for 10 minutes, gradually adding small amounts of the remaining flour, until the dough is smooth and elastic.

Place in an oiled bowl and brush the surface with oil. Cover with plastic wrap and leave in a warm place for 30 minutes, or until doubled in size.

To make the topping, heat the oil in a saucepan. Add the garlic and onion and cook, covered, over low heat for about 40 minutes, stirring frequently. The onion should be softened but not browned. Uncover and cook, stirring frequently, for another 30 minutes, or until lightly golden. Take care not to burn. Allow to cool.

Put the tomatoes in a saucepan and cook over medium heat, stirring frequently, for 20 minutes, or until thick and reduced to about 1 cup. Remove from the heat and stir in the concentrated tomato purée and herbs. Season to taste. Cool, then stir into the onion mixture.

Preheat the oven to 425°F. Punch down the dough, then turn out onto a floured surface and knead for 2 minutes. Divide in half. Return one half to the bowl and cover. Roll the other out to a 12 inch circle and press into the sheet. Brush with olive oil. Spread half the onion and tomato mixture evenly over the dough, leaving a small border. Arrange half the anchovy fillets over the top in a lattice pattern and place an olive in each square. Repeat with the rest of the dough and topping. Bake for 15–20 minutes, or until the dough is cooked through and lightly browned.

Tomato and Bocconcini Tart

1 1/2 cups) all-purpose flour

1/3 cup butter, chopped

1 egg

2 tablespoons iced water

5–6 plum tomatoes

salt, to sprinkle

1 tablespoon olive oil

8 (about 7 3/4 oz) fresh baby mozzarella
   cheese (bocconcini), sliced

6 scallions, chopped

2 tablespoons chopped rosemary

Combine the flour and butter in a food processor. Process for 10 seconds, or until fine and crumbly. Combine the egg and water in a small bowl. With the motor constantly running, gradually add to the flour mixture and process until the mixture just comes together. Turn out onto a lightly floured surface and knead to form a smooth dough. Refrigerate, covered, with plastic wrap, for 20 minutes.

Preheat the oven to 425°F. On a floured board, roll the pastry to fit a 9 inch round, loose-based tart pan. Ease the pastry into the pan and trim the edges. Cut a sheet of parchment paper to cover the pastry-lined pan. Place over the pastry, then spread a layer of baking beads or uncooked rice evenly over the paper. Bake for 15 minutes, then remove the paper and beads and bake for another 10 minutes, or until the pastry case is lightly golden, then cool. Reduce the oven to 350°F.

Cut the tomatoes in half, sprinkle with salt, and drizzle with the oil. Place in an ovenproof dish, cut side up, and bake for 15 minutes. Arrange the tomatoes, cut side up, over the pastry. Place the baby mozzarella slices and scallion between the tomatoes. Scatter with rosemary and season. Bake for 10 minutes. Remove from the oven and cool for 10 minutes before serving.

Goat's Cheese Galette

🌼 SERVES 6

🌼 PREPARATION TIME: 20 MINUTES

🌼 COOKING TIME: 1 HOUR 15 MINUTES

PASTRY

1 cup plain all-purpose flour

$^1/_4$ cup olive oil

FILLING

1 tablespoon olive oil

2 medium onions, thinly sliced

1 teaspoon thyme

$^1/_2$ cup ricotta cheese

$^1/_4$ cup goat's cheese

2 tablespoons pitted niçoise olives

1 egg, beaten

$^1/_4$ cup whipping cream

To make the pastry, sift the flour and a pinch of salt into a bowl and make a well in the center. Add the olive oil and mix with a flat-bladed knife until crumbly. Gradually add $^1/_4 - ^1/_3$ cup water until the mixture comes together. Remove and pat together to form a disc. Refrigerate for 30 minutes.

Meanwhile, to make the filling, heat the oil in a frying pan. Add the onion, cover and cook for 30 minutes. Season and stir in half the thyme. Cool.

Preheat the oven to 350°F. Lightly flour the workbench and roll out the pastry to a 12 inch circle. Then put on a heated baking sheet. Evenly spread the onion over the pastry, leaving a $^3/_4$ inch border. Sprinkle the ricotta and goat's cheese evenly over the onion. Put the olives over the cheeses, then sprinkle with the remaining thyme. Fold the pastry border in to the edge of the filling, pleating as you go.

Combine the egg and cream, then pour over the filling. Bake in the lower half of the oven for 45 minutes, or until the pastry is golden.

Mushroom, Asparagus and Feta Tart

🌸 SERVES 4

🌸 PREPARATION TIME: 30 MINUTES

🌸 COOKING TIME: 25 MINUTES

1 lb 2 oz block ready-made puff pastry, thawed

2 tablespoons oil

4$\frac{1}{2}$ cups sliced white mushrooms

3$\frac{1}{2}$ oz thin asparagus spears, woody ends trimmed

2 tablespoons chopped Italian parsley

1$\frac{1}{2}$ cups chopped feta cheese

Divide the pastry into two and roll each portion between two sheets of parchment paper. If making four tartlets, cut out two 4$\frac{1}{2}$ inch circles of pastry from each portion, or for two long tartlets roll each portion of pastry into a rectangle 4$\frac{1}{2}$ x 10 inches. Preheat the oven to 400°F.

Heat the oil in a frying pan, add the mushroom and asparagus, and stir until softened. Remove from the heat and add the parsley and feta. Stir and season. Spoon onto the pastry bases, leaving a $\frac{5}{8}$ inch border. Bake in the top half of the oven for 10–15 minutes, or until risen and brown. Serve warm or hot.

Sour Cream Tomato Pizza

* SERVES 4
* PREPARATION TIME: 30 MINUTES
* COOKING TIME: 40 MINUTES

1 teaspoon dried yeast
1 teaspoon superfine sugar
2 cups all-purpose flour
$1/2$ cup olive oil

TOPPING
$1/2$ cup sour cream
$1/3$ cup ricotta cheese
2 tablespoons chopped herbs (such as
   basil, lemon thyme, sage)
2 tablespoons oil
2 onions, thinly sliced
5 ripe tomatoes, sliced
2 garlic cloves, thinly sliced
$1/4$ cup marinated niçoise olives
10 lemon thyme sprigs

Preheat the oven to 400°F. To make the base, put the yeast, sugar, and $2/3$ cup warm water into a bowl and mix to dissolve the sugar. Leave in a warm, draught-free place for 10 minutes, or until bubbles appear on the surface. The mixture should be frothy and slightly increased in volume. If your yeast doesn't foam, it is dead, so you will have to discard it and start again.

Put the flour and a pinch of salt into a food processor, add the oil and the yeast mixture with the motor running, and process until it forms a rough dough. Turn out onto a lightly floured surface and knead until smooth. Place in a lightly oiled bowl, cover, and allow to rest in a warm area for $1 1/2$ hours, or until doubled in size. Punch down the dough and remove from the bowl. Knead and roll out to a 12 inch circle, or four $5 1/2$ inch circles and place on a non-stick baking sheet.

To make the topping, combine the sour cream, ricotta, and herbs. Spread over the pizza base, leaving a $1/2$ inch border.

Heat the oil in a frying pan, add the onions and cook for 10 minutes, or until caramelized. Cool slightly, spoon over the ricotta mixture and top with the tomato, garlic, olives, lemon thyme, and some freshly cracked black pepper. Bake in the top half of the oven for 15–30 minutes, depending on size, until the base is crisp and golden.

Turkish Pizza

❋ MAKES 8
❋ PREPARATION TIME: 25 MINUTES
❋ COOKING TIME: 45 MINUTES

1 teaspoon dried yeast
1/2 teaspoon sugar
1 1/2 cups all-purpose flour
1/3 cup olive oil
9 oz onions, finely chopped
1 lb 2 oz ground lamb
2 garlic cloves
1 teaspoon ground cinnamon
1 1/2 teaspoons ground cumin
1/2 teaspoon cayenne pepper
1/4 cup concentrated tomato purée
1 2/3 cups canned good-quality crushed
    tomatoes
1/3 cup pine nuts
3 tablespoons chopped cilantro leaves
Greek-style yogurt, to serve

Mix the yeast, sugar, and 1/4 cup warm water in a bowl. Leave in a warm, draught-free place for 10 minutes, or until bubbles appear on the surface. The mixture should be frothy and slightly increased in volume. If your yeast doesn't foam, it is dead, so you will have to discard it and start again.

Sift the flour and 1 teaspoon salt into a bowl, stir in the yeast mixture, 1 tablespoon of the oil and 3 1/2 fl oz warm water. Mix to form a soft dough, then turn onto a floured board and knead for 10 minutes, or until smooth. Place in an oiled bowl, cover, and leave in a warm place for 1 hour, or until doubled in size.

Heat 2 tablespoons of the oil in a frying pan over low heat and cook the onion for 5 minutes, or until soft but not golden. Add the lamb and cook for 10 minutes, or until brown. Add the garlic and spices, tomato purée and tomato. Cook for 15 minutes, until quite dry. Add half the pine nuts and 2 tablespoons of the coilantro. Season, then leave to cool.

Preheat the oven to 425°F. Grease two baking sheets.

Knock down the dough, then turn out onto a floured surface. Form into eight portions and roll each into a 4 1/2 x 7 inch oval. Place on the sheets. Divide the lamb mixture evenly among them and spread, leaving a small border. Sprinkle with the remaining pine nuts. Brush the edges with oil. Roll the uncovered dough over to cover the outer edges of the filling. Pinch the sides together at each end. Brush with oil. Bake for 15 minutes, or until golden. Sprinkle with the remaining cilantro, and serve with yogurt.

Crab Quiche

PASTRY

1¾ cups all-purpose flour

⅓ cup chilled butter, chopped

2 tablespoons iced water

FILLING

1 tablespoon butter

1 onion, thinly sliced

7 oz canned crabmeat, drained

3 eggs

¾ cup whipping cream

¾ cup grated cheddar cheese

dill sprigs (optional)

To make the pastry, sift the flour into a bowl. Using your fingertips, rub in the butter until the mixture resembles fine breadcrumbs. Make a well in the center and add the iced water. Mix with a flat-bladed knife, using a cutting action, until the mixture comes together in beads. Add a little more water if the dough is too dry. Turn out onto a lightly floured work surface and gather into a ball. Divide the pastry into two portions. Cover with plastic wrap and refrigerate for 20 minutes. Preheat the oven to 375°F. Grease two 4½ inches round, 1½ inches deep tart pans.

Roll out both portions of pastry between two sheets of parchment paper to fit the pans. Lift the pastry into the pans and press it well into the sides. Trim off any excess by rolling a rolling pin across the top of the pan. Refrigerate the pastry for 20 minutes. Cover the shells with parchment paper, fill evenly with baking beads or uncooked rice and bake for 15 minutes, or until the pastry is dried out and golden. Remove the paper and beads and cool slightly. Reduce the oven to 350°F.

To make the filling, melt the butter in a small frying pan and cook the onion until just soft. Remove from the pan and drain on paper towels. Squeeze out any excess moisture from the crabmeat. Spread the onion and crabmeat over the cooled pastry cases, arranging the crab in the center of each quiche. Mix the eggs, cream and cheddar in a bowl. Pour into the pastry cases and, if you like, top with some dill sprigs. Bake for 40 minutes, or until lightly golden and set.

Feta and Olive Herb Pie

🔥 SERVES 4–6
🔥 PREPARATION TIME: 40 MINUTES
🔥 COOKING TIME: 45 MINUTES

PASTRY

1 teaspoon sugar
2 teaspoons dried yeast
1 tablespoon olive oil
1/2 cup all-purpose flour
1 cup self-raising flour

FILLING

1 tablespoon olive oil
1 onion, sliced
1 teaspoon sugar
1/3 cup Italian parsley, chopped
1 rosemary sprig, chopped
3 thyme sprigs, chopped
5 basil leaves, torn
1/4 cup pine nuts, toasted (see Note)
1 garlic clove, crushed
1 1/4 cups feta cheese, crumbled
1/4 cup pitted olives, chopped

Dissolve half the sugar in 125 ml 1/2 cup warm water and sprinkle the yeast over the top. Leave in a warm, draught-free place for 10 minutes, or until bubbles appear on the surface. If your yeast doesn't foam, it is dead and you will have to start again. Mix the yeast mixture with the oil.

Sift the flours and 1/2 teaspoon salt into a large bowl. Make a well in the center and pour in the yeast mixture. Mix well and knead on a lightly floured board until smooth. Cut the dough in half, then roll each half into an 8 inch circle. Place one circle on a lightly greased baking sheet, the other on a baking sheet covered with parchment paper. Cover the circles with a dish towel and put in a warm place for 10–15 minutes, or until doubled in size. Preheat the oven to 400°F.

To make the filling, heat the oil in a frying pan, add the onion and for 10 minutes, or until golden brown. Sprinkle with the remaining sugar and cook for a further 5 minutes, or until caramelized. Transfer to a bowl and mix with the herbs, pine nuts, garlic, feta, and olives. Spread the mixture over the pastry on the greased sheet. Brush the edge with water and put the second pastry circle on top, using the paper to help lift it over. Press the edges together to seal and pinch together to form a pattern. Cut a few slits in the top of the pastry to allow steam to escape. Bake for 30–35 minutes, or until crisp and golden brown. Serve warm, cut into wedges.

NOTE: To toast pine nuts, you can dry-fry them in a frying pan, stirring and watching them constantly so they don't burn.

Herbed Fish Tartlets

🌸 MAKES 8
🌸 PREPARATION TIME: 40 MINUTES
🌸 COOKING TIME: 45 MINUTES

PASTRY

1 1/4 cups) all-purpose flour
1/3 cup butter, chopped
1 tablespoon chopped thyme
1 tablespoon chopped dill
2 tablespoons chopped Italian parsley
2/3 cup finely grated cheddar cheese
1/4–1/3 cup iced water

FILLING

14 oz skinless firm white fish fillets
2 scallions, finely chopped
2 tablespoons chopped Italian parsley
1/2 cup finely grated cheddar cheese
2 eggs
1/2 cup whipping cream

Lightly grease eight 4 inch round fluted tart pans. Sift the flour into a large bowl. Using your fingertips, rub in the butter until the mixture resembles fine breadcrumbs. Stir in the herbs and cheddar. Make a well in the center. Add almost all the water and mix with a flat-bladed knife, using a cutting action, until the mixture comes together in beads. Add more water if the dough is too dry. Gather together and form into a ball. Wrap in plastic wrap and refrigerate for 15 minutes.

Preheat the oven to 425°F. Divide the pastry into eight portions. Roll each on a lightly floured work surface, large enough to fit the pans. Ease into the pans, pressing into the sides. Trim the edges with a sharp knife or by rolling a rolling pin across the tops of the pans. Place the pans on a baking sheet. Cover each pastry case with a sheet of parchment paper. Spread a single layer of baking beads or uncooked rice evenly over the base. Bake for 10 minutes, then remove the paper and beads, and bake for another 10 minutes, or until lightly browned. Cool.

To make the filling, put the fish in a frying pan and add enough water to cover. Bring to a boil, reduce the heat, and simmer gently for 3 minutes. Remove from the pan with a slotted spoon and drain on crumpled paper towels. Allow to cool, then flake with a fork. Divide among the cases and sprinkle with the combined scallion, parsley, and cheddar. Whisk together the eggs and cream, then pour over the fish. Bake for 25 minutes, or until set and golden brown. Serve immediately.

NOTE: Smoked fish can be used. You can make the recipe in a a 9 inch tart pan. Cooking time may be longer; check after 25 minutes.

Potato and Onion Pizza

☀ SERVES 4
☀ PREPARATION TIME: 40 MINUTES
☀ COOKING TIME: 45 MINUTES

2 teaspoons dried yeast
½ teaspoon sugar
1½ cups bread flour
1 cup whole-wheat all-purpose flour
1 tablespoon olive oil

TOPPING
1 large red bell pepper
1 medium potato
1 large onion, sliced
1 cup soft goat's cheese, crumbled
    into small pieces
¼ cup capers
1 tablespoon dried oregano
1 teaspoon olive oil

Mix the yeast, sugar, a pinch of salt and 1 cup warm water in a bowl. Leave in a warm, draught-free place for 10 minutes, or until bubbles appear on the surface. The mixture should be frothy and slightly increased in volume. If your yeast doesn't foam, it is dead, so you will have to discard it and start again.

Sift both flours into a bowl. Make a well in the center, add the yeast mixture and mix to a firm dough. Knead on a lightly floured surface for 5 minutes, or until smooth. Place in a lightly oiled bowl, cover with plastic wrap or a damp dish towel and leave in a warm, draught-free place for 1–1½ hours, or until doubled in size.

Preheat the oven to 400°F. Brush a 12 inch pizza sheet with oil. Punch down the dough and knead for 2 minutes. Roll out to a 14 inch round. Put the dough on the sheet and tuck the edge over to form a rim.

To make the topping, cut the red pepper into large flattish pieces and remove the membrane and seeds. Place, skin side up, under a hot broiler until blackened. Cool in a plastic bag, then peel away the skin and cut the flesh into narrow strips.

Cut the potato into paper-thin slices and arrange over the base with the red pepper, onion and half the cheese. Sprinkle with the capers, oregano and 1 teaspoon cracked pepper and drizzle with oil. Brush the crust edge with oil and bake for 20 minutes. Add the remaining cheese and bake for 15–20 minutes, or until the crust has browned. Serve in wedges.

Moroccan Chicken Pie

🌸 SERVES 6–8

🌸 PREPARATION TIME: 30 MINUTES

🌸 COOKING TIME: 1 HOUR 20 MINUTES

¾ cup butter

3 lb 5 oz chicken, cut into 4 portions

1 large onion, finely chopped

3 teaspoons ground cinnamon

1 teaspoon ground ginger

2 teaspoons ground cumin

¼ teaspoon cayenne pepper

½ teaspoon ground turmeric

½ teaspoon saffron threads soaked in
    2 tablespoons warm water

½ cup chicken stock

4 eggs, lightly beaten

½ cup chopped cilantro

3 tablespoons chopped Italian parsley

⅓ cup chopped almonds

¼ cup confectioners' sugar

16 sheets filo pastry

confectioners' sugar, extra, to dust

Preheat the oven to 350°F. Grease a 12 inch pizza sheet.

Melt 2⅔ tablespoons butter of the butter in a large frying pan. Add the chicken, onion, 2 teaspoons of the cinnamon, all the other spices and the stock. Season, cover and simmer for 30 minutes, or until the chicken is cooked through.

Remove the chicken from the sauce. When cool enough to handle, remove the meat from the bones, discard the skin and bones and shred the meat into thin strips.

Bring the liquid in the pan to a simmer and add the eggs. Cook the mixture, stirring constantly, until the eggs are cooked and the mixture is quite dry. Add the chicken, chopped cilantro and parsley, season well and mix. Remove from the heat.

Bake the almonds on a baking sheet until golden brown. Cool slightly, then blend in a food processor or spice grinder with the icing sugar and remaining cinnamon until they resemble coarse crumbs.

Melt the remaining butter. Place a sheet of filo on the pizza sheet and brush with melted butter. Place another sheet on top in a pinwheel effect and brush with butter. Continue brushing and layering until you have used eight sheets. Put the chicken mixture on top and sprinkle with the almond mixture.

Fold the overlapping filo over the top of the filling. Place a sheet of filo over the top and brush with butter. Continue to layer buttered filo over the top in the same pinwheel effect until you have used eight sheets. Tuck the overhanging edges over the pie to form a neat round parcel. Brush well with the remaining butter. Bake the pie for 40–45 minutes, or until cooked through and golden. Dust with icing sugar before serving.

index

A

ajo blanco 27
anchovies
  pissaladière 277
  tapenade and anchovy tartlets 265
artichokes
  Russian salad 77
  stuffed artichokes 69
Asian oysters 165
asparagus
  asparagus with citrus hollandaise 79
  mushroom, asparagus and feta tart 283
avgolemono soup with chicken 47
avocado
  crab cakes with avocado salsa 123
  nachos with guacamole 91

B

beans
  mussels with black beans and coriander 155
  nachos with guacamole 91
  pasta and bean soup 23
  tuna, green bean and onion salad 105
beef
  carpaccio 173
  larb 195
  teppan yaki 181
  Thai beef salad 113
beet, fresh, and goat's cheese salad 103
blue cheese tagliatelle 227
bourride 35
brandade de morue 151
broccoli, orecchiette with 221
butter, clarifying 185

C

cabbage rolls 201
Caesar salad 89
California rolls 157
carpaccio 173
carrots
  carrot and cilantro soup 17
  spiced carrot and feta gnocchi 243
cheese
  blue cheese tagliatelle 227
  cheese and mushroom pies 265
  cheese tortellini with nutty herb sauce 253
  fennel risotto balls with cheesy filling 249
  gorgonzola and toasted walnuts on linguine 219
  haloumi with salad and garlic bread 83
  prosciutto, camembert and fig salad 93
  spinach and ricotta gnocchi 255

tomato and bocconcini tart 279
tomato and bocconcini salad 67
tomato and cheese risotto cakes 229
see also feta; goat's cheese
chef's salad 73
cherry tomato and pesto tart 275
chicken
  avgolemono soup with chicken 47
  chicken ballottine 177
  chicken, veal and mushroom loaf 189
  Chinese chicken and corn soup 59
  Circassian chicken 191
  Moroccan chicken pie 297
  spicy chicken broth with cilantro pasta 15
  tom kha gai 33
chicken livers
  chicken liver and Grand Marnier pâté 179
  tagliatelle with chicken livers and cream 245
chilled soba noodles 109
chili
  clams in chili paste 133
  coconut shrimp with chili dressing 143
  spaghettini with garlic and chili 253
Chinese chicken and corn soup 59
Circassian chicken 191
clams
  clams in chili paste 133
  clams in white wine 147
  New England clam chowder 21
  spaghetti clams 247
coconut
  coconut shrimp with chili dressing 143
  crab and mango salad 85
  tom kha gai 33
  winter squash, prawn and coconut soup 57
cold vegetable salad with spice dressing 97
corn
  Chinese chicken and corn soup 59
  corn chowder 39
  crab and corn eggflower noodle broth 27
  creamy corn and tomato soup 51
  turkey and corn soup 51
crab
  crab cakes with avocado salsa 123
  crab and corn eggflower noodle broth 27
  crab and mango salad 85
  crab quiche 289
  stuffed crab 153
cream of oyster soup 17
creamy corn and tomato soup 51
creamy red lentil soup 61
crepes, Vietnamese, with pork, shrimp and noodles 205

croustades
  shrimp 147
  tomato and basil 111
custard, savoury egg 197

D

duck
  duck breast with wild rice 187
  Peking duck with mandarin pancakes 207
  watercress and duck salad with lychees 93
dumplings, meat, in yogurt sauce 185

E

eggplant
  fish Wellington 263
  teppan yaki 181
eggs
  savoury egg custard 197
  stuffed shrimp omelettes 139

F

fast melon salad 73
fennel
  fennel risotto balls with cheesy filling 249
  salmon and fennel salad 75
  spaghetti with sardines, fennel and tomato 215
feta
  baked shrimp with feta 125
  feta and olive herb pie 291
  spiced carrot and feta gnocchi 243
  sweet potato, feta and pine nut strudel 261
fettucine
  creamy shrimp with fettucine 231
  fettucine alfredo 211
  fettucine with zucchini and crisp-fried basil 227
fish
  bourride 35
  brandade de morue 151
  fish and herb salad 81
  fish Wellington 263
  fried whitebait 135
  garlic, pasta and fish soup 13
  herbed fish tartlets 293
  lemon, herb and fish risotto 213
  smoked cod tart 273
  stuffed sardines 145
  see also salmon; seafood; tuna
French onion soup 13
frisée and garlic crouton salad 103

G

gado gado 87
garlic
  frisée and garlic crouton salad 103

garlic bucatini 239
garlic and ginger shrimp 131
garlic herb butter 217
garlic, pasta and fish soup 13
garlic shrimp 125
garlic soup 53
haloumi with salad and garlic bread
    83
snails with garlic and herb butter 199
spaghettini with garlic and chili 253
gazpacho, red 11
gnocchi
    gnocchi Romana 237
    parsnip gnocchi 217
    spiced carrot and feta gnocchi 243
    spinach and ricotta gnocchi 255
goat's cheese
    fresh beet and goat's cheese salad
        107
    goat's cheese galette 281
gorgonzola and toasted walnuts on linguine
    219
gravlax with mustard sauce 119
green papaya salad 95
green pea soup 39

H
haloumi with salad and garlic bread 83
harissa 31
herb-filled ravioli with sage butter 223
herbed fish tartlets 293

K
kebabs, rosemary tuna 129

L
lamb
    cabbage rolls 201
    crispy lamb with lettuce 183
    layered lamb and bulgur 203
    Turkish pizza 287
larb 195
lemon, herb and fish risotto 213
lemon-scented broth with tortellini 53
lentils
    creamy red lentil soup 61
    spinach and lentil soup 63
lettuce
    crispy lamb with lettuce 183
    san choy bau with noodles 193
linguine pesto 247
liver, sweet and sour 175
lobster
    lobster bisque 29
    lobster with parsley mayonnaise 127
    lobster thermidor 135

M
marinated salmon strips 161
marinated seafood 121
meat dumplings in yogurt sauce 185
melokhia soup 31
melon salad, fast 73
mixed vegetable salad 79
Moroccan chicken pie 297
moules marinière 167
mushrooms
    cheese and mushroom pies 265
    chicken, veal and mushroom loaf 189
    mushroom, asparagus and feta tart 283
    mushroom risotto 235
    pie-crust mushroom soup 37
    rissoni and mushroom broth 25
    stuffed mushrooms 75
mussels
    moules marinière 167
    mussels with black beans and cilantro 155
    zuppa di cozze 41
mustard sauce 119

N
nachos with guacamole 91
New England clam chowder 21
niçoise, salad 71
noodles
    chilled soba noodles 109
    pork noodle salad 99
    san choy bau with noodles 193

O
octopus, barbecued 137
omelettes, stuffed shrimp 139
onions
    French onion soup 13
    pissaladière 277
    potato and onion pizza 295
orecchiette with broccoli 221
orecchiette with tuna, lemon and caper sauce
    231
oysters
    Asian oysters 165
    cream of oyster soup 17
    oysters with bloody Mary sauce 119
    oysters in potatoes with cheese sauce
        127

P
pakoras, vegetable 115
panzanella 101
papaya
    green papaya salad 95
    prawn and papaya salad with lime
        dressing 107

pappa al pomodoro 23
parsnip gnocchi 217
pasta
    blue cheese tagliatelle 227
    cheese tortellini with nutty herb sauce
        253
    creamy shrimp with fettucine 231
    fettucine alfredo 211
    fettucine with zucchini and crisp-fried
        basil 227
    garlic bucatini 239
    garlic, pasta and fish soup 13
    gorgonzola and toasted walnuts on
        linguine 219
    lemon-scented broth with tortellini 53
    linguine pesto 247
    orecchiette with broccoli 221
    orecchiette with tuna, lemon and caper
        sauce 231
    pasta and bean soup 23
    pasta and spinach timbales 255
    penne alla Napolitana 233
    spicy chicken broth with cilantro pasta 15
    tagliatelle with chicken livers and cream
        245
    see also spaghetti
pâté, chicken liver and Grand Marnier 179
peanut sauce 87
peas
    green pea soup 39
    risi e bisi 239
    spicy tomato and pea soup 19
Peking duck with mandarin pancakes 207
penne alla Napolitana 233
Pepper
    red pepper soup 43
    roast pepper rice tarts 267
pie-crust mushroom soup 37
pies
    cheese and mushroom pies 265
    feta and olive herb pie 291
    free-form shrimp pies 275
    Moroccan chicken pie 297
pine nuts, toasting 261
pissaladière 277
pistou 55
pizza
    potato and onion 295
    sour cream tomato pizza 285
    Turkish pizza 287
pork
    larb 195
    pork noodle salad 99
    san choy bau with noodles 193
    Vietnamese crepes with pork, prawns and
        noodles 205

potatoes
  brandade de morue 151
  oysters in potatoes with
    cheese sauce 127
  potato and onion pizza 295
prosciutto, camembert and fig salad 93

Q
quail in vine leaves 175
quiche, crab 289

R
raita 115
ravioli
  creamy seafood ravioli 251
  herb-filled ravioli with sage butter 223
red gazpacho 11
red wine risotto 219
rice
  California rolls 157
  risi e bisi 239
  roast pepper rice tarts 267
risi e bisi 239
risotto
  fennel risotto balls with cheesy filling, 249
  lemon, herb and fish risotto 213
  mushroom risotto 235
  red wine risotto 219
  scallops on Asian risotto cakes with pesto,
    225
  tomato and cheese risotto cakes 229
rissoni and mushroom broth 25
rosemary tuna kebabs 129
Russian salad 77

S
sage butter 223
salads
  Caesar salad 89
  chef's salad 73
  cold vegetable salad with spice dressing
    97
  crab and mango salad 85
  fast melon salad 73
  fish and herb salad 81
  fresh beet and goat's cheese salad 107
  frisée and garlic crouton salad 103
  green papaya salad 95
  haloumi with salad and garlic bread 83
  mixed vegetable salad 79
  panzanella 101
  pork noodle salad 99
  prosciutto, camembert and fig salad 93
  Russian salad 77
  salad Niçoise 71
  salmon and fennel salad 75

shrimp and cucumber salad 67
shrimp and papaya salad with lime
  dressing 107
Thai beef salad 113
tomato and bocconcini salad 67
tuna, green bean and onion salad 105
watercress and duck salad with lychees 93
salmon
  gravlax with mustard sauce 119
  marinated salmon strips 161
  salmon and fennel salad 75
san choy bau with noodles 193
sardines, stuffed 145
scallops
  creamy baked scallops 149
  scallop ceviche 165
  scallops on Asian risotto cakes with pesto
    225
  scallops Provençale 169
  scallops with soba noodles and dashi
    broth 49
seafood
  Asian oysters 165
  barbecued octopus 137
  clams in chili paste 133
  clams in white wine 147
  crab cakes with avocado salsa 123
  crab quiche 289
  cream of oyster soup 17
  creamy baked scallops 149
  creamy seafood ravioli 251
  lobster bisque 29
  lobster with parsley mayonnaise 127
  lobster thermidor 135
  marinated seafood 121
  moules marinière 167
  mussels with black beans and cilantro
    155
  oysters with bloody Mary sauce 119
  oysters in potatoes with cheese sauce 127
  scallop ceviche 165
  scallops Provençale 169
  seafood quenelles 141
  seafood terrine 159
  spaghetti marinara 241
  spaghetti clams 247
  squid with green peppercorns 163
  stuffed crab 153
  zuppa di cozze 41
  see also fish; shrimp
shrimp
  baked shrimp with feta 125
  coconut shrimp with chili dressing 143
  creamy shrimp with fettucine 231
  free-form shrimp pies 275
  garlic and ginger shrimp 131

garlic shrimp 125
san choy bau with noodles 193
shrimp and basil soup 25
shrimp bisque 49
shrimp cocktails 151
shrimp croustade 161
shrimp and cucumber salad 67
shrimp and papaya salad with lime
  dressing 107
stuffed shrimp omelettes 139
Vietnamese crepes with pork, shrimp and
  noodles 205
winter squash, shrimp and coconut soup
  57
silverbeet, chicken ballottine 177
smoked cod flan 273
snails with garlic and herb butter 199
soba noodles, chilled 109
soup
  ajo blanco 27
  avgolemono soup with chicken 47
  bourride 35
  carrot and cilantro soup 17
  Chinese chicken and corn soup 59
  corn chowder 39
  crab and corn eggflower noodle broth 27
  cream of oyster soup 17
  creamy corn and tomato soup 51
  creamy red lentil soup 61
  French onion soup 13
  garlic, pasta and fish soup 13
  garlic soup 53
  green pea soup 39
  lemon-scented broth with tortellini 53
  lobster bisque 29
  melokhia soup 31
  New England clam chowder 21
  pappa al pomodoro 23
  pasta and bean soup 23
  pie-crust mushroom soup 37
  red pepper soup 43
  red gazpacho 11
  rissoni and mushroom broth 25
  scallops with soba noodles and dashi
    broth 49
  shrimp and basil soup 25
  shrimp bisque 49
  soupe au pistou 55
  spicy chicken broth with cilantro pasta
    15
  spicy tomato and pea soup 19
  spinach and lentil soup 63
  tofu miso soup 59
  tom kha gai 33
  turkey and corn soup 51
  watercress soup 45

wild rice soup 45

winter squash, shrimp and coconut soup 57

winter squash soup with harissa 31

won ton soup 63

yogurt soup 33

zuppa di cozze 41

soupe au pistou 55

soupe au pistou 55

sour cream tomato pizza 285

spaghetti

spaghetti carbonara 211

spaghetti with creamy lemon sauce 221

spaghetti marinara 241

spaghetti puttanesca 233

spaghetti with sardines, fennel and tomato 215

spaghetti clams 247

spaghettini with garlic and chili 253

spicy chicken broth with cilantro pasta 15

spicy tomato and pea soup 19

spinach

pasta and spinach timbales 255

spinach and lentil soup 63

spinach and ricotta gnocchi 255

squid

grilled squid 137

squid with green peppercorns 163

sweet potato, feta and pine nut strudel 261

sweet and sour liver 175

T

tagliatelle with chicken livers and cream 245

tapenade and anchovy tartlets 265

tarts

cherry tomato and pesto tart 275

herbed fish tartlets 293

mushroom, asparagus and feta tart 283

roast capsicum rice tarts 267

smoked cod tart 273

tapenade and anchovy tartlets 265

tomato and bocconcini tart 279

winter squash tarts 259

teppan yaki 181

Thai beef salad 113

tofu miso soup 59

tom kha gai 33

tomatoes

cherry tomato and pesto tart 275

creamy corn and tomato soup 51

pappa al pomodoro 23

penne alla Napolitana 233

pissaladière 277

sour cream tomato pizza 285

spicy tomato and pea soup 19

tomato and basil croustades 111

tomato and bocconcini tart 279

tomato and bocconcini salad 67

tomato and cheese risotto cakes 229

tomato coulis 141

Turkish pizza 287

tuna

niçoise, salad 71

orecchiette with tuna, lemon and caper sauce 231

rosemary tuna kebabs 129

tuna, green bean and onion salad 105

Tunisian brik 271

turkey and corn soup 51

Turkish pizza 287

V

vegetables

asparagus with citrus hollandaise 79

cold vegetable salad with spice dressing 97

mixed vegetable salad 79

stuffed artichokes 69

stuffed mushrooms 75

vegetable pakoras 115

Vietnamese crepes with pork, shrimp and noodles 205

vol-au-vents 269

W

walnuts

Circassian chicken 191

gorgonzola and toasted walnuts on linguine 219

watercress

watercress and duck salad with lychees 93

watercress soup 45

whitebait, fried 135

wild rice

duck breast with wild rice 187

wild rice soup 45

winter squash

winter squash, prawn and coconut soup 57

winter squash soup with harissa 31

winter squash tarts 259

won ton soup 63

Y

yogurt sauce 185

yogurt soup 33

Z

zuppa di cozze 41

This 2009 edition published by Fall River Press,
by arrangement with Murdoch Books Pty Limited.

Chief Executive: Juliet Rogers
Publishing Director: Kay Scarlett

Editor: Jacqueline Blanchard
Design concept: Heather Menzies
Design layout: Joanna Byrne and Wendy Inkster
Photographer: Jared Fowler
Stylist: Cherise Koch
Production: Alexandra Gonzalez

Fall River Press
122 Fifth Avenue
New York, NY 10011

ISBN: 978-1-4351-1045-8

Printed and bound in Malaysia

1 3 5 7 9 10 8 6 4 2

IMPORTANT: Those who might be at risk from the effects of salmonella poisoning (the elderly, pregnant women, young children
and those suffering from immune deficiency diseases) should consult their doctor with any concerns about eating raw eggs.

OVEN GUIDE: You may find cooking times vary depending on the oven you are using. For fan-forced ovens,
as a general rule, set the oven temperature to 35°F lower than indicated in the recipe.

Some of the recipes in this book have appeared in *Cooking Essentials*.